D0132084

Wei-Chuan Cooking School was founded in 1961 as a subsidiary of Wei-Chuan Food Corporation, the largest food manufacturer in Taiwan. The school soon became the largest and most respected institution of its kind along the Asia-Pacific rim. Graduates included world-class chefs, institutional teachers, professional caterers, connoisseurs of Chinese cuisine as well as many homemakers.

As Wei-Chuan's reputation grew, requests came from all over the world for guidance and information relative to the recipes used in the cooking classes. In an effort to meet this demand, *Chinese Cuisine* was written and published in 1972. The book was very successful and became the first in a series of Wei-Chuan Cookbooks. Wei-Chuan Publishing was founded later that same year in Taipei with a branch subsequently established in the U.S.A. in 1978.

Wei-Chuan Cookbooks are now recognized as the most comprehensive books in the Chinese cuisine field. Wei-Chuan's current plans include new books covering cuisines from all over the world. *Thai Cooking Made Easy* and *Mexican Cooking Made Easy* are examples of this expansion.

Wei-Chuan's success can be attributed to its commitment to provide the best quality product possible. Almost all recipes are complemented by full color photographs. Each recipe is written simply with easy-to-follow instructions and precisely measured ingredients. Wei-Chuan stands behind its name, reputation, and commitment to remain true to the authenticity of its recipes.

異國風味

泰國菜
THAI
COOKING MADE EASY

齊舒肯 Sukhum Kittivech

味全
WeiChuan

作者：齊舒肯
盤飾：齊娃比

總編輯：黃淑惠
翻譯：張超琰
文稿編輯：林淑華、賴燕貞、何久恩
文稿協助：殷宗寧

攝影：大野現
設計編輯：張方馨
封面設計：曲靜
內頁設計：王瑾

印刷者：中華彩色印刷股份有限公司

出版者：味全出版社有限公司
台北市仁愛路四段28號2樓
郵政劃撥0018203-8號　黃淑惠帳戶
TEL：2702-1148・2702-1149
FAX：2704-2729

版權所有：局版台業字第0179號
1992年10月初版
2000年11月7版　7-8-5

定價：新台幣貳佰捌拾元整

AUTHOR: Sukhum Kittivech
FOOD STYLIST: Vavy Kittivech

CHIEF EDITOR: Su-Huei Huang
TRANSLATOR: Wynne Chang
EDITORIAL STAFF: Sophia Lin,
Yen-Jen Lai, John Holt
COLLABORATOR: Lynette In.

PHOTOGRAPHER: Aki Ohno
ART DIRECTION: F. Chang
COVER DESIGN: Jean Chu
BOOK DESIGN: Chin Ong

WEI-CHUAN PUBLISHING
1455 Monterey Pass Rd., #110
Monterey Park, Ca 91754, U.S.A.
Tel：(323) 261-3880・(323) 261-3878
Fax：(323) 261-3299

WEI-CHUAN PUBLISHING CO., LTD.
2nd FL., 28 Section 4, Jen-Ai Road
Taipei, Taiwan
Tel：(02) 2702-1148・2702-1149
Fax：(02) 2704-2729

PRINTED IN TAIWAN
By China Color Printing Co., Ltd.

目錄

Contents

齊舒肯於1970年代初期由泰國移居美國，隨後以他在泰國多年的烹調經驗，即與本食譜盤飾負責人齊娃比在南加州共同創立了"千達拉"泰國餐館，開張後深受好評；短短二年內又陸續成立了另2家連鎖"千達拉"餐館。

由於齊舒肯親自督導餐館內外，使"千達拉"能一直維持泰國菜的水準及傳統的精緻口味，成為南加州最受歡迎的泰國餐館之一。多年來不斷有顧客詢問有關泰國菜的做法，為應付廣大群眾的需求，"泰國菜"一書終將付梓，深信讀者採用此書後，在家享用異國風味的泰式佳餚，將不再是奢望。

Sukhum (Ken) Kittivech came to the U.S.A. from Thailand in the early 1970's, and brought with him an extensive knowledge in authentic Thai cooking. Shortly after his arrival he, together with his partner Vavy, opened the first Chan Dara restaurant in Southern California. The popularity of his exotic cuisine grew rapidly, and within a few years two additional Chan Daras were opened to the public.

In order to maintain the high standards and delicate flavors of his meals, Sukhum personally guides every chef at each restaurant location, in his culinary art. As a result of this dedication to perfection and authenticity, all Chan Daras are considered among the finest Thai restaurants in Southern California. Because of this, numerous requests are continually received from diners at all restaurants. From these requests, the idea to create *Thai Cooking Made Easy* was born.

Sukhum wants you to enjoy the wide range of carefully selected modern and traditional recipes in this book, with the knowledge that each dish can be easily and successfully prepared at home.

序 泰國菜是經由中國、印度、印尼、越南及泰國本土的飲食文化交流後，綜合產生的獨特餐飲。因其菜餚具有酸、甜、辣味的獨特風格，深受一般人喜愛。讀者使用本食譜時，若能依據以下原則來選擇菜餚，即可在家享用美味的泰國餐。

1 選擇烹飪方式不同的菜餚。

2 選擇不同種類、不同色彩的材料，如肉、海鮮、蔬菜的搭配使素、葷均衡，且色彩優美。

3 選擇不同口味如酸、甜、辣味等，使每道菜有不同風格。

一餐通常可選用3-5道菜的組合，例如講究的 2 人份餐，可選用烤牛肉片(前菜)、洋芋雞腿咖哩、蛋包什錦及白飯，4 人份以炸海鮮餅(前菜)、酸辣白菜湯、玉米筍炒雞肉、泰式牛排再配以白飯。

用餐時將所有菜放在餐桌中央，每一盤菜上置一湯匙，以供大家將食物盛至自己盤內。泰國菜進食時餐具一般使用叉子及湯匙，筷子多用於麵食。

Introduction
Thai Cuisine finds its roots in the historical blending of Chinese, Indian, Indonesian, Vietnamese and Thai cultures. The popularity of Thai cuisine has grown dramatically all over the world because of the exotic contrasts in taste of the sweet, sour and hot dishes in a typical meal. Adherence to the following principles when preparing Thai cuisine will provide well balanced and deliciously tasteful home-style or formal meals.

1 Select recipes utilizing different cooking methods.

2 Choose ingredients from different food groups and colors to create delightfully tasty and balanced combinations. For example, meat, poultry, or seafood with vegetables.

3 Select dishes which will offer the sour, sweet and hot contrasts in taste.

A traditional Thai meal usually consists of a combination of three to five dishes. For example, a typical two person meal, may consist of Thai BBQ Beef (appetizer), Chicken & Red Curry, Thai Stuffed Omelet, and rice. A four person meal may consist of Fried Shrimp Cake (appetizer), Spicy Nappa Cabbage Soup, Chicken & Baby Corn, Thai Steak, and rice. Readers should feel free to exercise flexibility and change the dishes according to the above three principles and individual preferences.

Customarily, the dishes (each containing a spoon) are simultaneously placed in the center of the table. When ready to dine, each person serves himself by using the spoon to scoop food onto his plate. The Thai people eat their meals with fork and spoon, using chopsticks only with noodle dishes.

Now it's time to prepare some exotic dishes, and experience the unparalleled enjoyment of authentic *Thai Cooking Made Easy*. Enjoy!

量器介紹 Conversion Table

1杯(1飯碗)＝16大匙
1 cup (1c.)＝236c.c.

1大匙(1湯匙)
1 Tablespoon (1T.)＝15c.c.
1斤＝600公克　1兩＝37.5公克

1小匙(1茶匙)
1 teaspoon (1t.)＝5c.c.

香菜介紹 Fragrant Spices & Herbs

1 泰國菜常使用的香菜包括──香茅、薄荷葉、泰國檸檬葉、芫荽、九層塔
(由左至右)，經常用在湯、炒、拌類、咖哩內，或當醃料使用，以增加菜餚之香味。

1 Lemon grass, mint leaves, Kaffir leaves, cilantro, and basil leaves(from left to right) are often used in Thai recipes.They are often added for extra flavor in soups, stir-fried dishes, tossed dishes, curry dishes, and seasoning sauces.

蔬菜切法 Cutting Vegetables

以下為數種常用切法。
1 切塊：如茄子、洋葱、生菜切塊。
2 切條：炒菜類常用切粗條。
3 切片：切薄片或切厚片，多用在湯、炒或拌類
4 切絲：辣椒絲、薑絲常用在炒類或湯內。
5 切粒：葱切粒又稱葱花，多用在炒類或湯內。
6 切碎：蒜切碎，簡稱蒜末，辣椒切碎，簡稱辣椒末，多用在炒類。

The following terms in this book apply as indicated:
1 Cut in pieces: Eggplant, onion, lettuce.
2 Cut in strips: Stir-fried dishes usually have vegetables cut in thick strips.
3 Slice: Thin or thick slices; often used in soups, stir-fried dishes, and tossed dishes.
4 Shred: Threads of chili and ginger root often used in stir-fried dishes or soups.
5 Chop: Small pieces of green onions used mainly in stir-fried dishes or soups.
6 Mince: Very small pieces of garlic and minced chili used mainly in stir-fried dishes.

調味料介紹
Seasoning Sauces

泰國菜內使用的調味料種類繁多，但材料準備齊全後，程序簡單易做，以下主要調味料，分六大類介紹：

Various seasoning sauces are used in Thai recipes. When the ingredients and sauces are assembled beforehand, the recipes are very easy to prepare. Major sauces used are described in 1 through 6 below.

1

2

3

4

1 甜醬油、鮮味露、蠔油、魚露、白醬油(左至右)，其中以魚露爲主要用料，有時用鮮味露或蠔油來調理菜餚之不同鮮味；甜醬油的作用是加深菜餚的顏色。故書內若同時使用白醬油(又稱淡醬油或生抽)及甜醬油時，可用普通醬油或黑醬油(老抽)取代。

2 青檸檬、酸子(左至右)等天然物爲泰國菜內常用的酸味來源。將酸子2oz與溫水1杯調勻，過濾後即成酸子汁，若無青檸檬可用檸檬取代。

3 黑糖、椰子糖(左至右)泰國菜調理甜味有時使用椰子糖，若無可用黑糖取代。

4 辣椒醬、辣椒膏、乾辣椒、大乾辣椒、綠辣椒(左至右)、辣椒粉(中下)爲泰國菜內常用辣味來源。乾辣椒與大乾辣椒另有不同風味。新鮮辣椒種類很多，本書內多使用綠辣椒。上列辣椒因辛辣不同，讀者可依喜好選用。

1 **Sweet Soy Sauce, Maggi Sauce, Oyster Sauce, Fish Sauce, Thin Soy Sauce** (also called light soy sauce) (from left to right). Fish sauce is the most used seasoning sauce. Sometimes maggi sauce or oyster sauce is used to achieve different flavor. Sweet soy sauce (caramel) is often used to enhance the color of a dish. Soy sauce or dark soy sauce may be substituted for both white and sweet soy sauce.

2 **Lime, Tamarind** (from left to right) are natural fruits often used for sour flavoring in Thai recipes. To make tamarind juice, mix well 2 oz. (56g) tamarind with 1 c. warm water then filter the mixture.

3 **Palm Sugar, Brown Sugar,** (from left to right). Palm sugar is sometimes used for sweet flavoring in Thai recipes. If palm sugar is not available, brown sugar may be used instead.

4 **Chili Paste, Chili Paste with Soya Oil, Dry Chili, Dried New Mexican Chili, Green Chili** (from left to right), **Chili Powder** (middle below) are often used as hot flavoring spices in Thai recipes. Dry chili and dried New Mexican chili provide different flavors. There are many types of fresh chilies and the chilies described above may be substituted for one another, although green chili is used most often in this book.

5

6

5 潘納咖哩醬、紅咖哩醬、綠咖哩醬、瑪沙門咖哩醬、卡森咖哩醬爲本書內所使用代表性咖哩，其中以紅咖哩醬使用較多，各類咖哩可互相取代，市面上售有袋裝和罐裝，依其廠牌有不同的包裝。

6 椰子粉、椰奶(左至右)椰奶用來煮咖哩菜餚或加入湯內，可買現成或自製(如無椰奶，可用牛奶取代)。椰奶做法：椰子粉1杯加溫水1½杯用果汁機攪爛，篩子過濾後，可製一杯椰奶。若冷藏會浮上一層濃汁稱椰奶漿。

5 **Panang Curry Paste, Red Curry Paste, Green Curry Paste, Masaman Curry Paste,** and **Kang Som Curry Paste** are the major curry pastes used in this book. Of these, red curry paste is used most often. Different curry pastes may be substituted for one another. Curry pastes are sold in bags and in cans. Different brands may pack differently.

6 **Desiccated Coconut, Coconut Milk** (from left to right). Ready-made or homemade coconut milk is used for cooking curry dishes or as an addition to soups. If coconut milk is not available, substitute with milk. To make coconut milk: Stir well 1 c. desiccated coconut with 1½ c. warm water in a blender then filter through sifter to make 1 c. coconut milk. The foam floating on top after refrigerating is called thick coconut milk.

副的調味料目的是用來增加菜餚的香味，可隨喜好酌量加入菜餚內。
The following minor seasonings add extra flavor to dishes. Season to personal preference.

1 碎米 買現成或將米炒成金黃色後搗碎。

2 碎花生 將花生搗碎。

3 蒜油 將蒜末與油炒香後即成蒜油。

4 蝦粉 買現成或將蝦米切碎成粉。

1 **Ground Rice:** Ready-made ground rice is available in most markets, or can be prepared by frying rice until color changes to golden brown then grinding into fine pieces.

2 **Ground Peanuts:** Grind peanuts into fine pieces.

3 **Garlic Oil:** Stir-fry minced garlic in oil until fragrant.

4 **Shrimp Powder:** Ready-made shrimp powder is available in most markets, or can be prepared by mincing dry shrimp.

1

2

3

4

沾料介紹
Dipping Sauces

酸、甜、辣味是泰國菜的獨特風味，以下數種可用於沾料或與菜餚配食。
The special flavors of Thai dishes include sour, sweet, and hot. The following sauces can be used for dipping or served with various dishes.

牛排沾料
Thai Steak Sauce

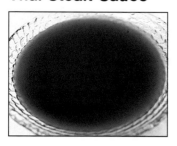

①	乾辣椒	2條
	小番茄	4粒
	洋蔥切片	¼杯

②	魚露	3大匙
	青檸檬汁	2大匙
	水	½小匙

①	2 dried chilies
	4 cherry tomatoes
	¼ c. sliced onion

②	3 T. fish sauce
	2 T. lime juice
	½ t. water

1 將①料以小火炒至略焦黑後與②料入果汁機內攪爛即成。
● 此沾料多用在沾牛排及烤肉。

1 Stir-fry ① until slightly burned then liquify with ② in a blender.
● This sauce is excellent for dipping steak and B.B.Q. meat.

海鮮沾料
Tamarind Sauce

| ① | 魚露、椰子糖 | 各2大匙 |
| | 酸子汁（見8頁） | 3大匙 |

| ② | 蒜、辣椒末 | |
| | 洋蔥絲、碎花生 | 適量 |

| ① | 2 T. ea: fish sauce, palm sugar |
| | 3 T. tamarind juice (P.8) |

| ② | minced garlic, minced chili, shredded onion and crushed peanuts as desired |

1 將①料燒開煮1分鐘，待涼後成濃汁，食時隨意加②料。
● 此沾料適合於沾烤魚、蝦、龍蝦等海鮮類。

1 Bring ① to boil then cook 1 minute; let cool to form thick juice. When serving, ② may be added as desired.
● This sauce is a favorite for dipping seafood such as fish, shrimp, and lobster.

花生調味沾料
Peanut Sauce

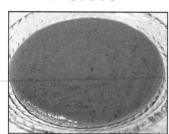

①	咖哩	1小匙
	魚露、花生醬	各2大匙
	酸子汁（見8頁）、糖	各3大匙
	紅椒粉、蒜粉	各1小匙
	椰奶	2杯
	碎花生	4大匙

①	1 t. masaman curry paste
	2 T. ea: fish sauce, peanut butter
	3 T. ea: tamarind juice (P.8), sugar
	1 t. ea: paprika powder, garlic powder
	2 c. coconut milk.
	4 T. crushed peanuts.

1 將①料燒開後，改中火邊攪邊煮15分鐘至汁剩1½杯。
● 此種特別口味的沾料是用來拌雞絲沙拉用。

1 Bring ① to boil; stir 15 minutes in medium heat until liquid is reduced to 1½ c.
● This special dipping sauce goes well with chicken salad.

辣椒醋、辣椒魚露

Chili Vinegar Sauce, Chili Fish Sauce

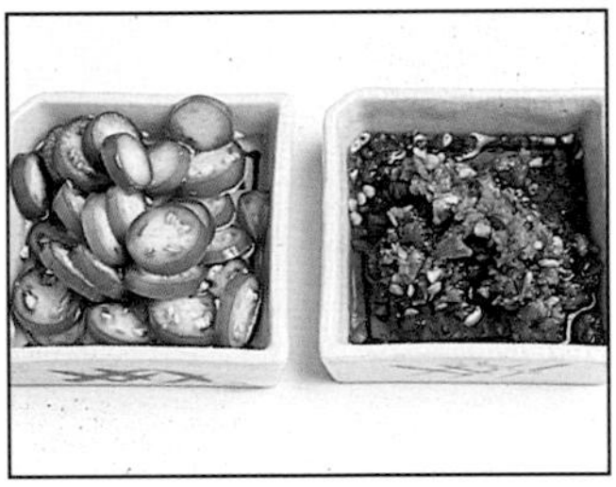

1 醋加辣椒粒成辣椒醋(左)或魚露、青檸檬汁加辣椒粒成辣椒魚露(右)(可隨意加糖)此爲一般日常沾料，可與各類菜餚、麵、炒飯等配食。

1 Add vinegar with chopped chilies to make chili vinegar sauce (left). Add fish sauce, lime juice with chopped chilies to make chili fish sauce (right) (may add sugar as desired). These popular dipping sauces are used daily in Thailand with various dishes, noodles, or fried rice.

烤肉沾料

Thai B.B.Q. Sauce

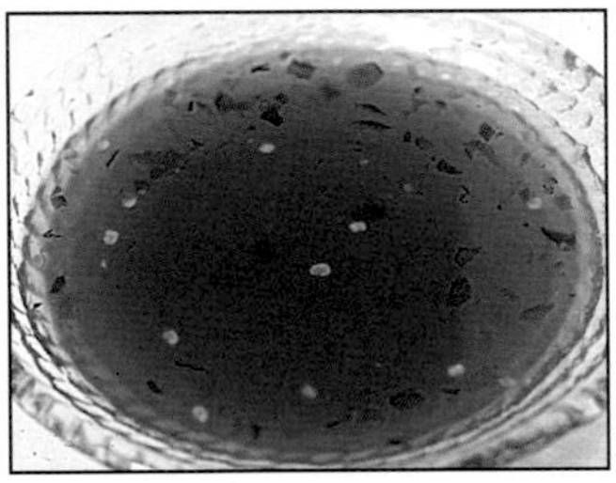

1	蒜末	1小匙	1	**1 t. minced garlic**
	辣椒或辣椒醬	½小匙		**½ t. minced chili or chili paste**
	糖、水	各4大匙		**4 T. ea: sugar, water**
	塩	¼小匙		**¼ t. salt**
	醋	6大匙		**6 T. vinegar**

1 將1料燒開後，煮5分鐘至汁剩6大匙，待涼後成薄汁。

● 此爲沾泰國烤雞大家喜愛的沾料

1 Bring 1 to boil then cook 5 minutes until liquid is reduced to 6 T. Let cool to form thin juice.

● This is a popular dipping sauce for B.B.Q. chicken in Thai cuisine.

涼拌黃瓜、涼拌甜黃瓜

Cucumber Sauce, Sweet Cucumber Sauce

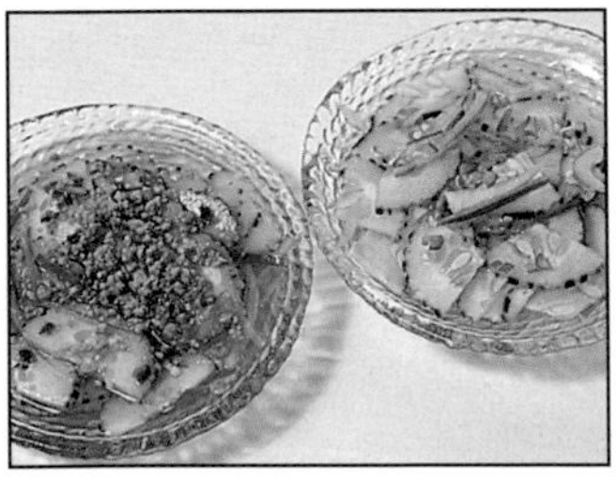

1	糖、醋	各4大匙	1	**4 T. ea: sugar, vinegar**
	塩	¼小匙		**¼ t. salt**
	水	2大匙		**2 T. water**
2	黃瓜(切片)	¼條	2	**¼ cucumber, sliced**
	洋葱(切絲)	⅙個		**⅙ onion, shredded**

1 將1料燒開待涼，加入2料即成涼拌黃瓜，如在1料內多加2大匙糖，2料內多加適量的辣椒，上撒碎花生即成涼拌甜黃瓜。

● 此二種黃瓜，可任意與各種菜餚配食。但炸類菜餚特別適合與涼拌甜黃瓜配食。

1 Bring 1 to boil then let cool. Add 2 to make cucumber sauce. To make sweet cucumber sauce, add an additional 2 T. sugar to 1, chilies to 2 then sprinkle on crushed peanuts.

● These two cucumber sauces are popular with many dishes. The sweet sauce is especially tasty with deep-fried dishes.

雞絲沙拉
Chicken Salad

雞胸肉 ·········· 3兩
熟蛋(切塊) ·········· 1個

<u>1</u>
生菜(切塊) ·········· 4片
黃瓜、紅蘿蔔(切片)···各¼個
番茄(切片) ·········· ½個
洋葱絲 ·········· ¼杯

¼ lb. (115g) boneless chicken breast
1 hard-boiled egg, cut in pieces

<u>1</u>
4 leaves of lettuce, cut in pieces
¼ ea (sliced): cucumber, carrot
½ sliced tomato
¼ c. shredded onion

1 水燒開，隨入肉煮熟(約15分鐘)，撈出待涼後，撕成絲。

2 將雞絲、蛋及<u>1</u>料置盤，酌量淋上「花生調味沾料」(見10頁)配食。

● <u>1</u>料見圖1。

1 Cook breast in boiling water 15 minutes. Remove and let cool then tear in shreds.

2 Place shreds, egg, and <u>1</u> on plate; pour on "peanut sauce" (P.10). Serve.

● See Fig.1 for <u>1</u>.

Fig.1

Fig.2

Fig.3

檸檬碎豬肉
Ground Pork in Lime Juice (Nam)

1. 豬絞肉 ························· 6兩
   豬皮(見12頁，圖3) ······ ¼杯
2. 2料同下
3. 洋蔥絲 ·························¼杯
   蔥花、芫荽末 ········ 各1大匙
   薑絲 ·························1大匙

1. ½ lb. (225g) ground pork
   ¼ c. shredded pork skin
   (Fig.3, P.12)
2. see 2 in below recipe
3. ¼ c. shredded onion
   1 T. ea (chopped): green
   onion, cilantro
   1 T. shredded ginger

1 將2料燒開，再入1料攪開至變色，拌入3料，可與喜好蔬菜配食。

● 如無豬皮時可免用。菜內若加花生2大匙，可增加香味。

1 Heat 2 in a small pan; add and stir 1 until separated and color changes. Mix with 3. May be served with favorite vegetables.

● The pork skin in 1, if not available, may be omitted. 2 T. peanuts may be added for extra flavor.

檸檬碎牛肉
Ground Beef in Lime Juice (Larb)

1. 牛絞肉 ························· 6兩
2. 魚露、青檸檬汁 ······ 各2大匙
   糖 ·····························¼小匙
   辣椒粉 ·······················1小匙
3. 洋蔥絲 ·························¼杯
   蔥花 ·························1大匙
   薄荷葉(略切) ··············12片

1. ½ lb. (225g) ground beef
2. 2 T. ea: fish sauce, lime juice
   ¼ t. sugar
   1 t. ground chili
3. ¼ c. shredded onion
   1 T. chopped green onion
   12 mint leaves, chopped

1 將2料燒開，再入絞肉攪開至變色，拌入3料，可與喜好蔬菜配食。

● 菜內若加碎米1大匙(見12頁，圖2)可增加香味。

1 Heat 2 in a small pan; add 1 and stir until separated and color changes. Mix with 3. May be served with favorite vegetables.

● 1 T. ground rice sticks (Fig.2, P.12) may be added for extra flavor.

鳳梨碎肉
Pineapple Delight (Ma Haw)

新鮮或罐裝鳳梨塊(圖1)⋯1杯
豬絞肉 ⋯⋯⋯⋯⋯⋯⋯⋯ 4兩

1 | 蒜末、芫荽末 ⋯⋯⋯⋯ 各1小匙
  | 洋葱末 ⋯⋯⋯⋯⋯⋯⋯ 1大匙

2 | 魚露 ⋯⋯⋯⋯⋯⋯⋯⋯ 1½大匙
  | 青檸檬汁、酸子汁 各1½大匙
  | 椰子糖 ⋯⋯⋯⋯⋯⋯⋯ 1¾大匙

碎花生(見9頁)⋯⋯⋯⋯⋯2大匙

3 | 芫荽、紅辣椒絲⋯⋯⋯⋯適量

1 c. fresh or canned
   pineapple pieces (Fig.1)
⅓ 1b. (150g) ground pork

1 | 1 t. minced garlic
  | 1 t. minced cilantro
  | 1 T. minced onion

2 | 1½ T. ea: fish sauce, lime
  | juice, tamarind juice
  | 1¾ T. palm sugar

2 T. crushed peanuts (P.9)

3 | cilantro & shredded red
  | chili as desired

1 油2大匙燒熱，炒香 1 料，隨入肉炒至變色，依序入 2 料及碎花生拌炒後，
　鏟出待涼。

2 將炒好的肉與 3 料置於鳳梨塊上即成。

● 此菜可當聚會的前菜。

1 Heat 2 T. oil then stir-fry 1 until fragrant. Add meat and stir-fry
  until color changes. Add 2 and crushed peanuts; stir to mix.
  Remove and let cool.

2 Place meat over pineapple pieces; then sprinkle with 3 . Serve.

● This dish makes a great appetizer.

Fig. 1

豬肉沙拉

Pork Salad (Yum Yai)

豬肉(切片) ················· 3兩
蝦(無殼) ················· 3兩
乾木耳(泡軟) ·············¼杯
熟蛋 ····················· 1個

1 糖 ····················· 2大匙
水 ····················· 1大匙

2 魚露 ················· 2½大匙
青檸檬汁 ··············· 3大匙
辣椒醬(圖1)、蒜末···各1小匙

3 生菜(切塊) ·············· 3片
黃瓜·····················12片
洋蔥絲······················¼杯

¼ **lb. (115g) sliced pork**
¼ **lb. (115g) shelled shrimp**
¼ **c. dried wood ears,**
   softened in cold water
1 hard boiled egg

1 2 **T. sugar**
1 **T. water**

2 2½ **T. fish sauce**
3 **T. lime juice**
1 **t. chili paste (Fig.1)**
1 **t. minced garlic**

3 3 **leaves of lettuce, cut in**
   pieces
12 **cucumber slices**
¼ **c. shredded onion**

1 蝦抽去腸泥，洗淨後瀝乾水份。蛋去殼，蛋白切碎，蛋黃壓碎。

2 將 1 料燒開，隨入蛋黃及 2 料攪拌成沙拉汁。

3 肉、蝦及木耳分別在滾水內燙熟，依序拌入沙拉汁與 3 料，撒上蛋白即成。

● 肉、蝦見圖2。

1 Devein shrimp; rinse and drain. Remove egg shell; chop egg white and mash egg yolk.

2 Bring 1 to boil; add egg yolk and 2, stir to make salad dressing.

3 Cook meat, shrimp, then wood ear separately in boiling water. Remove, then mix with salad dressing then 3. Sprinkle with egg white; serve.

● See Fig.2 for meat and shrimp.

Fig. 1

Fig. 2

臘腸沙拉
Thai Sausage

中式香腸(圖1)⋯⋯⋯⋯2條

1️⃣ 魚露、青檸檬汁 ⋯⋯ 各1大匙
糖、辣椒末 ⋯⋯⋯⋯ 各1小匙

2️⃣ 黃瓜片、洋蔥絲 ⋯⋯ 共1½杯
薑絲 ⋯⋯⋯⋯⋯⋯⋯⋯ 2大匙
芫荽⋯⋯⋯⋯⋯⋯⋯⋯⋯適量

2 Chinese sausages (Fig.1)

1️⃣ 1 T. fish sauce
1 T. lime juice
1 t. ea: sugar, minced chili

2️⃣ total of 1½ c.: sliced
cucumbers, shredded
onions
2 T. shredded ginger
cilantro as desired

1 香腸烤熟後，斜切薄片備用；將 1️⃣ 、 2️⃣ 料翻拌後再入香腸即成。

● 香腸用烤或煎均可。中式香腸拌入泰式調味料及生菜，即成別緻的前菜。

1 Cook sausages then cut diagonally in thin pieces. Set aside. Stir to mix 1️⃣ and 2️⃣ then mix with sausages.

● Depending on personal preference, sausage may be either baked or fried. To make that special Thai appetizer, mix Chinese sausage with Thai seasonings and lettuce.

Fig. 1

魚片沙拉
Cat Fish Salad

魚肉（切塊）⋯⋯⋯⋯⋯ 8兩

1 | 薑絲、蝦米（圖1）⋯⋯ 各⅔兩

炸油⋯⋯⋯⋯⋯⋯⋯⋯適量

洋葱丁、青檸檬丁⋯⋯各¼杯
2 | 辣椒（切丁）⋯⋯⋯⋯⋯ 3條
花生⋯⋯⋯⋯⋯⋯⋯⋯⅔兩

生菜 ⋯⋯⋯⋯⋯⋯⋯⋯ 6片

⅔ 1b. (300g) fish, cut in pieces

1 | 1 oz. (28g) ea: shredded ginger, dried shrimp (Fig.1)

oil for deep-frying

2 | ¼ c. ea (Chopped): onion, lime
3 chopped chilies
1 oz. (28g) peanuts

6 leaves of lettuce

1 魚用炭火或烤箱烤熟，也可用油煎熟；1料炸呈金黃色即撈出，置於紙巾上吸油。

2 食用時，每片生菜內放入適量的魚，1料及2料，淋上「海鮮沾料」（見10頁）包捲而食。

● 炸過的薑絲與蝦米味香，再配上有酸辣口味的2料，是一道別緻的家常或宴客菜餚。

1 Fish may be grilled, oven baked, or fried in oil. Deep-fry 1 until golden; remove and place on paper towel to absorb oil.

2 When serving, place fish, 1, and 2 on lettuce leaf; spread on some "tamarind sauce" (P.10) , then roll up.

● Deep-fried ginger shreds and shrimps, when served with hot and sour flavored 2, is a special dish for home or party.

Fig. 1

鮪魚沙拉
Tuna Salad

鮪魚(吐哪)1罐⋯⋯⋯⋯6兩

1 | 魚露、青檸檬汁 ⋯⋯ 各1大匙
　 | 糖、辣椒末 ⋯⋯⋯⋯ 各1小匙

2 | 芹菜、洋葱(切絲) ⋯ 共1½杯
　 | 葱花，香茅(切碎) ⋯ 各1大匙
　 | 薄荷葉⋯⋯⋯⋯⋯⋯⋯12片

½ 1b. (225g) canned tuna

1 | 1 T. fish sauce
　 | 1 T. lime juice
　 | 1 t. ea: sugar, minced chili

2 | total of 1½ c. (shredded):
　 | 　onions, celery
　 | 1 T. chopped green onion
　 | 1 T. minced lemon grass
　 | 12 mint leaves

1 鮪魚瀝去水份備用，將1、2料翻拌後再拌入鮪魚即成。

● 做好的鮪魚沙拉與飯配食外，可放在小餅乾上，做爲一道宴客時的開胃菜；或與生菜夾入麵包內成爲經濟可口的三明治午餐。

● 香茅的處理法：需先去除老皮，上端較嫩的部份切碎，用在沙拉內、下段較老的部份切段用在湯內。

1 Drain tuna set aside. Stir 1 and 2 then mix with tuna. Serve.

● Tuna salad may be served with rice or placed on small crackers as an appetizer; or with lettuce on bread for a delicious sandwich.

● Preparing lemon grass: Trim off the hard skin. Mince the upper tenderer portion. Cut the lower harder portion in pieces for soups.

海鮮沙拉
Spicy Shrimp & Squid Yum

蝦仁、魷魚 ·············· 共6兩

① 魚露、青檸檬汁 ··· 各1½大匙
糖、辣椒粉 ·········· 各1小匙
蒜油··························¼小匙

② 洋蔥絲·····················¼杯
葱絲、香茅(切碎) ··· 各1大匙
薄荷葉·····················12片

total of ½ lb. (225g)
shelled shrimp & squid

① 1½ T. ea: fish sauce, lime
juice
1 t. ea: sugar, ground chili
¼ t. garlic oil

② ¼ c. shredded onion
1 T. ea: shredded green
onion, minced lemon
grass
12 mint leaves

1 蝦抽去腸泥,洗淨後瀝乾水份。魷魚去除薄膜,洗淨後在內面劃交叉刀痕,並切塊(見50頁,圖2)。

2 蝦仁、魷魚分別在滾水內川燙至捲起即撈出,依序拌入①、②料,可與喜好蔬菜配食。

● 注意:在燙蝦、魷魚時,煮太久鮮味會流失。

1 Devein shrimp; rinse and drain. Peel off membrane from squid's hood. Rinse squid then make cross diagonal cuts to form diamond-shapes on inside surface; cut in pieces (Fig. 2, see P.50).

2 Add shrimp and squid to boiling water and cook until curled; remove then mix with ① and ②. May be served with favorite vegetables.

● To maintain their flavors, do not overcook shrimp and squid.

烤蝦沙拉
Naked Shrimp

蝦（無殼） ···················· 6兩

1   魚露、靑檸檬汁 ··· 各1½大匙
      糖、辣椒末 ·········· 各1小匙
      辣椒膏或沙茶醬········½小匙

2   洋葱絲·····················¼杯
      薄荷葉·····················12片

½ 1b. (225g) shelled
     shrimp

1   1½ T. ea: fish sauce, lime
     juice
     1 t. ea: sugar, minced chili
     ½ t. chili paste with soya
     bean oil or barbecue
     (Sa Tsa) sauce

2   ¼ c. shredded onion
     12 mint leaves

1 蝦抽去腸泥，洗淨後瀝乾水份，由背部剖開，腹部仍相連，並在蝦肉面輕劃刀痕，以免烤時捲起。

2 蝦在炭火上烤至變色即熟，依序拌入 **1**、**2** 料，可與喜好的蔬菜配食。

● 如用烤箱，先將烤箱燒至500°F，大蝦兩面各烤約3分鐘，小蝦兩面各烤約2分鐘至變色即熟。

1 Devein shrimp; rinse and drain. Make a cut at the back of each shrimp to butterfly. Score the inside surface of each shrimp to prevent curling during cooking.

2 Grill shrimp until color changes. Mix with **1** then **2** . Serve with favorite vegetables.

● If using oven, preheat to 500°F. Bake large shrimp 3 minutes each side and small shrimp 2 minutes each side until color changes.

綠木瓜沙拉
Papaya Salad

1. 綠木瓜絲、紅蘿蔔絲(圖1)共3兩

2. 蒜 ························· 2瓣
   乾辣椒 ······················ 4條

3. 長豆(切段) ················· 3條
   小番茄(切半) ············· 3個

4. 魚露 ······················· 2大匙
   青檸檬汁 ··············· 1½大匙
   椰子糖、酸子汁 ······ 各1大匙
   碎花生、蝦粉(見9頁)各1大匙

1. total of ¼ 1b. (115g)
   (shredded): green Thai
   papaya, carrot (Fig.1)

2. 2 garlic cloves
   4 dry chilies

3. 3 long string beans, cut
   1″ (2cm) long
   3 cherry tomatoes, cut in
   half

4. 2 T. fish sauce
   1½ T. lime juice
   1 T. ea: palm sugar,
   tamarind juice
   1 T. ea: crushed peanuts,
   shrimp powder (P.9)

1 先將 2 料搗碎(圖2)，隨入 3 料略搗，續入 1 料翻拌後，再酌量加 4 料拌勻。

● 此種用綠木瓜做成的沙拉是最受泰國女士喜愛的沙拉。

1 Crush 2 (Fig.2); add 3 and crush briefly. Add 1 and stir to mix; then mix with 4 as desired.

● Salad, made with green Thai papaya, is the most popular salad dish of the Thai women.

Fig. 1

Fig. 2

粉絲沙拉

Bean Threads in Lime Juice (Yum Woon Sen)

1 | 豬絞肉，蝦（無殼）‥‥‥‥共6兩

2 | 草菇（圖1，罐頭）‥‥‥‥‥10個
乾木耳（圖2，泡軟）‥‥‥¼杯
乾粉絲（泡軟略切）‥‥‥‥2兩

3 | 魚露、靑檸檬汁‥‥‥‥各2大匙
糖、蒜末‥‥‥‥‥‥各½小匙
辣椒粉‥‥‥‥‥‥‥‥1小匙
水‥‥‥‥‥‥‥‥‥‥6大匙

4 | 洋蔥絲‥‥‥‥‥‥‥‥‥⅓杯
蔥花、碎腰果‥‥‥‥各2大匙
炸乾蝦米‥‥‥‥‥‥‥1大匙
薄荷葉‥‥‥‥‥‥‥‥‥適量

1 | total of ½ lb. (225g): ground pork, shelled shrimp

2 | 10 canned straw mushrooms (Fig.1)
¼ c. dried wood ears (Fig.2), softened in cold water
3 oz. (84g) dried bean threads, softened in cold water then cut in half

3 | 2 T. ea: fish sauce, lime juice
½ t. ea: sugar, minced garlic
1 t. ground chili
6 T. water

4 | ⅓ c. shredded onion
2 T. chopped green onions
2 T. crushed cashew nuts
1 T. dried shrimp, deep fried
mint leaves as desired

1 ①料內蝦抽去腸泥，洗淨後瀝乾水份。

2 半鍋水燒開，放入②料再燒開即撈出。

3 將③料燒開，放入①料邊煮邊攪至肉與蝦變色即熄火，依序拌入燙熟的②料及④料即成。

● 乾木耳¼杯泡軟後爲1杯。

1 Devein shrimp; rinse and drain.

2 Bring water to boil. Add ② and bring to another boil; remove ②.

3 Bring ③ to boil. Add ①; stir and cook until pork and shrimp change color. Turn off heat then mix with cooked ② then ④. Serve.

● When softened in cold water, ¼ c. dried wood ears will yield 1c.

Fig. 1

Fig. 2

香炸米粉
Sweet Crispy Noodles (Meekrob)

米粉 ························· 1兩
炸油························· 適量
蛋(打散) ··················· 1個
蝦(無殼) ··················· 4兩

1
魚露 ······················· 1大匙
醋 ························· 3大匙
酸子汁 ····················· 2大匙
糖 ························· 5大匙
紅椒粉(圖1)··············· 1小匙
醃蒜(圖2、切碎)········· 2大匙

豆芽 ······················· 3兩

1½ oz. (40g) rice sticks
oil for deep-frying
1 beaten egg
⅓ lb. (150g) shelled shrimp

1
1 T. fish sauce
3 T. vinegar
2 T. tamarind juice
5 T. sugar
1 t. paprika powder (Fig.1)
2 T. preserved garlic (Fig.2), minced

¼ lb. (115g) bean sprouts

1 蝦抽去腸泥,洗淨後瀝乾水份;米粉用手鬆開。

2 炸油燒熱,先取數條米粉放入油內,如沈底表示油溫度太低,如迅速浮起,可分次將米粉放入炸,浮起後撈出(溫度太高時,炸出的米粉焦黑)。餘油將蛋液慢慢倒入,用中火炸至金黃絲帶狀,撈出後置於紙巾上吸油後備用(圖3)。

3 油1大匙燒熱,將蝦炒至變色,依序入 1 料、米粉、蛋及豆芽輕拌均勻即成。

1 Devein shrimp; rinse and drain. Separate rice sticks by hand.

2 Heat oil for deep-frying; test temperature by putting in some rice sticks. If they sink to bottom, oil is not hot enough. If they float to top, put in several rice sticks at a time. Remove as threads float to top (If temperature is too high, sticks will burn). Repeat with remaining rice sticks until all sticks are fried. Slowly pour in egg. Deep-fry in medium heat until shreds become golden. Remove and place on paper towel to absorb oil (Fig.3).

3 Heat 1 T. oil then stir-fry shrimp until color changes. Add 1 , rice sticks, egg, and bean sprouts; stir to mix well. Serve.

Fig. 1

Fig. 2

Fig. 3

23

牛肉沙拉
Beef Salad

牛排(圖1)·················9兩

1
魚露、青檸檬汁 ······ 各2大匙
糖、蒜末················½小匙
辣椒末 ·················· 1小匙
洋葱末、碎米(見9頁)各1大匙
薄荷葉(切碎)············10片

¾ 1b. (340g) beef steak

1
2 T. fish sauce
2 T. lime juice
½ t. sugar
½ t. minced garlic
1 t. minced chili
1 T. ea: minced onion,
   ground rice (P.9)
10 mint leaves, minced

1 牛肉兩面各撒少許塩,在炭火上邊翻面邊烤至喜好的熟度;逆紋切片,拌入 **1** 料,與喜好的蔬菜配食。

● 如用烤箱,先將烤箱燒熱,肉置上層,烤箱門略開,以500°F烤(火由上往下)烤至喜好的熟度即成。

1 Sprinkle salt on both sides of beef. Grill beef until desired tenderness is reached (turn beef over several times during grilling). Slice beef across grain then mix with **1**. Serve with favorite vegetables.

●If using oven, preheat at broil to 500°F. Place meat near heat or flame. Broil meat with oven door slightly open.

Fig. 1

Fig. 2

Fig. 3

烤牛肉片
Thai B.B.Q. Beef

牛肉(切長片、見24頁,圖2)8兩

1	醬油、酒、麻油 …… 各1大匙
	胡椒 ……………………¼小匙
	糖、葱片、薑片……各½大匙

⅔ lb. (300g) beef sirloin, sliced (Fig.2, P.24)

1 — 1 T. ea: soy sauce, cooking wine, sesame oil
¼ t. pepper
½ T. sugar
½ T. ea (sliced): green onion, ginger

1 牛肉拌入 1 料醃1小時。

2 肉在炭火上邊翻面邊烤至喜好的熟度、沾「辣椒魚露」(見11頁)食用。

● 如用烤箱;先將烤箱燒熱,肉置上層,烤箱門略開,以500°F烤(火由上往下)烤至喜好熟度即成。

1 Marinate beef with 1 1 hour.
2 Grill meat until desired tenderness is reached (turn meat over several times during grilling). Serve with "chili fish sauce" (P.11).

● If using oven, preheat at broil to 500°F. Place meat near heat or flame. Broil meat with oven door slightly open until desired tenderness is reached.

泰式牛排
Thai Steak

紐約牛排1片(見24頁,圖3)9兩

1	魚露 …………………… 1大匙
	辣醬油 ………………… 1小匙
	糖、甜醬油…………各¼小匙
	青檸檬汁………………¾大匙
	蒜末、辣椒末、胡椒各½小匙
	洋葱末…………………½大匙

¾ lb. (340g) New York steak (Fig.3, P.24)

1 — 1 T. fish sauce
1 t. worcestershire sauce
¼ t. sugar
¼ t. sweet soy sauce
¾ T. lime juice
½ t. ea (minced): garlic, chili, pepper
½ T. minced onion

1 牛排拌入 1 料醃15分鐘。

2 牛排在炭火上邊翻面邊烤或用烤箱烤(見24頁)至喜好熟度,沾「牛排沾料」(見10頁)食用。

1 Marinate steak with 1 15 minutes.
2 Grill steak or use oven to broil (see P.24) until desired tenderness is reached (turn steak over several times during cooking). Serve with "Thai steak sauce" (P.10).

泰式烤雞
Thai B.B.Q. Chicken

雞半隻 ················· 1斤

魚露 ················· 2大匙
胡椒 ················· ½小匙
黃薑粉或咖哩粉 ······· ½小匙
椰奶或牛奶 ············ ½杯
蒜、芫荽莖(切碎) ··· 各1大匙

1

½ chicken, 1⅓ lb, (600g)

1

2 T. fish sauce
½ t. pepper
½ t. tumeric powder or
    curry powder
½ c. coconut milk or milk
1 T. ea (minced): garlic,
    cilantro roots

1 雞拌入 **1** 料醃 3 小時(圖1、2)。

2 雞在炭火上邊翻面邊烤至略焦,肉熟;切塊後沾「烤肉沾料」(見11頁)食用。

● 如用烤箱,先將烤箱燒熱,雞皮朝上,置烤盤上層,烤箱門略開,以500°F 烤(火由上往下)烤至表皮呈金黃色,再以400°F烤至雞熟共烤約50分鐘。

● 黃薑粉是用來加強菜色用。

1 Marinate chicken with **1** for 3 hours (Figs. 1 & 2).

2 Grill chicken until slightly burned (turn chicken over several times during grilling). Chop chicken to bite size pieces, then serve with "Thai B.B.Q. Sauce" (P. 11).

● If using oven, preheat at broil to 500°F. Place chicken near heat or flame with chicken skin facing up. Broil chicken with oven door slightly open until skin is golden. Reduce heat to 400°F and broil until done. Total broiling time is about 50 minutes.

● Tumeric powder is used to enhance the color.

Fig. 1

Fig. 2

Fig. 3

Fig. 4

烤豬排
B.B.Q. Pork Chops

豬排(見26頁,圖3) ····· 12兩

魚露 ···················· 1大匙
糖、甜醬油 ·········· 各1小匙
① 胡椒 ···················· ¼小匙
黃薑粉或咖哩粉 ········· ¼小匙
蒜、芫荽莖(切碎) ···各½大匙

椰奶或牛奶 ············· 3大匙

1 lb. (450g) pork chop (Fig.3, P.26)

1 T. fish sauce
1 t. sugar
1 t. sweet soy sauce
① ¼ t. pepper
¼ t. tumeric powder or curry powder
½ T. ea (minced): garlic, cilantro roots

3 T. coconut milk or milk

1 豬排拌入①料及椰奶醃2小時。

2 肉在炭火上邊翻面將二面烤熟,沾「烤肉沾料」(見11頁)食用。

● 如用烤箱;先將烤箱燒熱,肉置上層,烤箱門略開,以500˚F烤(火由上往下)二面各烤6分鐘,呈略焦狀即成。

1 Marinate pork with ① and coconut milk 2 hours.

2 Grill pork until cooked (turn pork over several times during grilling). Serve with "Thai B.B.Q. sauce" (P.11).

● If using oven, preheat at broil to 500˚F. Place meat near heat or flame. Broil meat, with oven door slightly open, 6 minutes on each side until slightly scorched.

串燒
Skewered B.B.Q Beef (Sate)

牛肉(雞肉或蝦) ············ 8兩

① ①料同上

椰奶 ······················ 4大匙
竹籤(20公分長) ··········· 10枝

⅔ lb. (300g) beef

① see ① on above recipes

4 T. coconut milk or milk
10 skewers, 8" (22cm) long

1 肉切寬2公分,長15公分薄片,拌入①料及椰奶醃1小時。

2 肉片用竹籤串起(見26頁,圖4),在炭火上邊翻面將二面烤至喜好熟度,沾「花生調味沾料」或與「涼拌黃瓜」(見11頁)配食。

● 如用烤箱;先將烤箱燒熱,肉置上層,烤箱門略開,以500F烤(火由上往下)烤8分鐘,呈略焦狀即成。

1 Cut meat in 1"×6"(2cm×15cm) slices then marinate with ① and milk 1 hour.

2 Insert skewers through meat slices (Fig.4, P.26) then grill until desired tenderness is reached (turn meat over several times during grilling). Serve with "peanut sauce" (P.10) or "cucumber sauce" (P.11).

● If using oven, preheat at broil to 500˚F. Place meat near heat or flame. Broil meat, oven door slightly open, 8 minutes until slightly scorched.

豉汁烤魚
Baked Rainbow Trout

鱒魚1條(圖1)⋯⋯⋯⋯⋯9兩

1
油⋯⋯⋯⋯⋯⋯⋯⋯2½大匙
蒜蓉豆豉醬(圖2)⋯⋯2½大匙
糖、胡椒⋯⋯⋯⋯各½小匙
蒜、薑、芫荽莖(切碎)各1大匙

¾ 1b. (340g) whole fish (Fig.1)

1
2½ T. ea: oil, black bean garlic sauce (Fig.2)
½ t. ea: sugar, pepper
1 T. ea (minced): garlic, ginger, cilantro roots

1 魚洗淨，拭乾水份，魚身二面各劃3刀，將拌好的**1**料均勻塗抹魚身，用鋁箔紙包住，上打洞。

2 烤箱燒至400°F，放入魚烤約40分鐘至熟即成。

● 魚由腹部切開，背部連接，打開成一片，可以節省烤的時間。拌料後的魚亦可用蒸或微波爐加熱至熟。

1 Rinse fish and pat dry; cut 3 lines vertically on both sides of fish. Spread mixture **1** evenly on fish then wrap with foil. Make holes in foil.

2 Preheat oven to 400°F. Bake fish 40 minutes until cooked. Serve.

● Cut fish along belly, do not cut through back. Open it out as one piece to shorten baking time. Fish with mixture **1** may be cooked by steaming or microwave oven.

Fig. 1

Fig. 2

Fig. 3

Fig. 4

辣味烤鱼
Grilled Sea Bass With Chili Sauce

魚肉(見28頁，圖3)········8兩

1
蒜、辣椒、芫荽莖(切碎)各½大匙
洋葱末 ················· 4大匙

2
魚露、酸子汁 ········ 各2大匙
糖 ···················· 1大匙
高湯(或水) ············· 4大匙

⅔ lb. (300g) fish fillet (Fig.1, P.28)

1
½ T. ea (minced): garlic, chili, cilantro roots
4 T. minced onion

2
2 T. fish sauce
2 T. tamarind juice
1 T. sugar
4 T. stock or water

1 魚兩面撒少許鹽，用炭火或烤箱烤熟，也可用油煎或微波爐煮熟。

2 油2大匙燒熱，炒香 1 料，隨入 2 料燒開，澆在烤好的魚肉上即成。

1 Sprinkle salt on both sides of fish then grill or oven bake until color changes. Fish may also be fried in oil or microwaved.

2 Heat 2 T. oil then stir-fry 1 until fragrant. Add 2 and bring to boil. Pour on grilled fish; serve.

薑味烤鱼
Grilled White Fish with Ginger Sauce

魚肉2片(見28頁，圖4) ··· 8兩

1
蒜末、辣椒末········各½大匙
豆瓣醬 ················ 1大匙

2
薑絲、葱絲·········· 各¼杯

3
白醬油 ·············· 1½大匙
糖、醋、太白粉 ····· 各1小匙
高湯(或水) ············ 5大匙

2 slices of fish, ⅔ lb. (300g) (Fig.4, P.28)

1
½ T. ea (minced): garlic, chili
1 T. soy bean condiment

2
¼ c. ea (shredded): ginger, green onions

3
1½ T. thin soy sauce
1 t. ea: sugar, vinegar, cornstarch
5 T. stock or water

1 魚兩面撒少許鹽，用炭火或烤箱烤熟，也可用油煎或微波爐煮熟。

2 油2大匙燒熱，炒香 1 料，入 2 料略炒後，再加調勻的 3 料勾汁，澆在烤好的魚肉上即成。

1 Sprinkle salt on both sides of fish then grill or oven bake until color changes. Fish may also be fried in oil or microwaved.

2 Heat 2 T. oil then stir-fry 1 until fragrant. Add 2 and stir-fry briefly. Add mixture 3 to thicken then pour on grilled fish. Serve.

炸雞肉餅

Deep-fried Chicken Cake (Chicken Tod Mun)

① 雞絞肉 ···················· 6兩
　 魷魚(剁碎)··············¼杯

② 紅咖哩醬 ············· 1½大匙
　 塩 ····················¼小匙
　 糖、太白粉 ·········· 各1小匙
　 蛋 ····················1個
　 泰國檸檬葉(切碎) ········ 2片
　 蘇打粉···············⅛小匙

　 四季豆(切粒) ·········· 3大匙
　 炸油·····················適量

① ½ 1b. (225g) ground chicken
　 ¼ c. ground squid

② 1½ T. red curry paste
　 ¼ t. salt
　 1 t. ea: sugar, cornstarch
　 1 egg
　 2 minced kaffir leaves
　 ⅛ t. baking soda

3 T. chopped string beans
oil for deep-frying

1 將①、②料用攪拌機或用手攪拌至有粘性,隨入四季豆拌勻。手沾水做成
　6個肉餅(圖1)。

2 炸油燒熱,中火將肉餅炸約5分鐘至熟,可與「涼拌甜黃瓜」(見11頁)配食。

1 Stir ① and ② until sticky (use food processor or hand). Add string beans and mix well. Dip hands in water then divide mixture in 6 mounds (Fig. 1).

2 Heat oil for deep-frying then fry the mounds in medium heat 5 minutes until cooked. May be served with "sweet cucumber sauce" (P. 11).

Fig. 1

Fig. 2

Fig. 3

乾煎雞翼
Heavenly Chicken Wings

雞翅	1斤
1 薑絲	2大匙
蒜末、辣椒末	各1大匙
泰國檸檬葉(切碎)	6片
2 魚露	2大匙
糖、醋	各2小匙
高湯(或水)	2大匙

1⅓ lbs. (600g) chicken wings

1
2 T. shredded ginger
1 T. ea (minced): garlic, chili
6 minced kaffir leaves

2
2 T. fish sauce
2 t. ea: sugar, vinegar

2 T. stock or water

1 雞翅洗淨,拭乾水份,切成二段(見30頁,圖2)。

2 油½杯燒熱,放入雞翅半煎炸約10分鐘二面呈金黃色,鏟於鍋邊。留油2大匙,炒香①料,依序入②料及雞翅拌炒後,再加高湯燒開即成。

1 Rinse chicken wings; pat dry then cut in 2 pieces (Fig.2, P.30).

2 Heat ½ c. oil then fry wings 10 minutes until golden on both sides. Move the wings to the side of the pan. Use 2 T. remaining oil to stir-fry 1 until fragrant. Add 2 then chicken wings; stir to mix. Add stock and bring to boil. Serve.

炸牛肉乾
Thai Beef Jerky

牛排(切長塊、見30頁,圖3)8兩	
1 白醬油、魚露	各¾大匙
糖	1小匙
胡椒	½小匙
洋蔥(切塊)	¼杯
炸油	適量

⅔ lb. (300g) flank steak, cut in ½″×3″×½″ (1cm×8cm ×1cm) pieces (Fig.3, P.30)

1
¾ T. thin soy sauce
¾ T. fish sauce
1 t. sugar
½ t. pepper

¼ c. onion pieces
oil for deep-frying

1 牛排拌入①料醃15分鐘。

2 炸油燒熱,中火將牛排、洋蔥同時炸至洋蔥變棕色,即撈出。可沾「牛排沾料」(見10頁)食用。

1 Marinate steak with 1 15 minutes.

2 Heat oil for deep-frying then deep-fry steak and onion in medium heat until onion is golden. Remove. May be served with "Thai steak sauce" (P.10).

炸海鮮餅
Fried Shrimp Cake (Shrimp Tod Mun)

[1] 蝦泥 ……………………… 6兩
　　魷魚(剁碎) ……………… ¼杯

[2] 白醬油 …………………… ¾大匙
　　胡椒、糖、太白粉…各½小匙
　　蛋 …………………………1個
　　芫荽莖(切碎) ………… 1大匙
　　蘇打粉 …………………… ⅛小匙

　　麵包粉 …………………… 1杯
　　炸油 …………………………適量

[1] **½ lb. (225g) ground shrimp**
　　¼ c. ground squid

[2] **¾ T. thin soy sauce**
　　½ t. ea: pepper, sugar,
　　　cornstarch
　　1 egg
　　1 T. minced cilantro roots
　　⅛ t. baking soda

1 c. bread crumbs
oil for deep-frying

1 將 [1]、[2] 料用攪拌機或用手攪拌至有粘性，手沾水做成6份蝦餅，兩面沾裹麵包粉(圖1)。

2 炸油燒熱，中火將蝦餅炸約5分鐘至熟，可與「涼拌甜黃瓜」(見11頁)配食。

1 Mix [1] and [2] thoroughly until sticky (by food processor or hand). Dip hands in water then divide the mixture in 6 mounds. Coat both sides of mounds with bread crumbs (Fig. 1).

2 Heat oil for deep-frying then fry shrimp cakes in medium heat 5 minutes until cooked. May be served with "sweet cucumber sauce" (P. 11).

Fig. 1

Fig. 2

土司鑲肉
Thai Toast

<table>
<tr><td>1</td><td>豬絞肉、蝦泥 ………… 共4兩</td></tr>
<tr><td rowspan="4">2</td><td>蛋 ………………………… 1個</td></tr>
<tr><td>葱花、芫荽末 ……… 各1大匙</td></tr>
<tr><td>魚露 ……………………… 2小匙</td></tr>
<tr><td>蒜粉、胡椒 ………… 各¼小匙</td></tr>
<tr><td></td><td>麵包 ……………………… 2片</td></tr>
<tr><td></td><td>炸油………………………… 適量</td></tr>
</table>

<table>
<tr><td>1</td><td>total of ⅓ lb. (150g): ground pork, ground shrimp</td></tr>
<tr><td rowspan="5">2</td><td>1 egg</td></tr>
<tr><td>1 T. ea (chopped): green onion, cilantro</td></tr>
<tr><td>2 t. fish sauce</td></tr>
<tr><td>¼ t. garlic powder</td></tr>
<tr><td>¼ t. pepper</td></tr>
<tr><td></td><td>2 slices of bread
oil for deep-frying</td></tr>
</table>

1 將 1、2 料用攪拌機或用手攪拌至有粘性，分別塗在麵包上(見32頁，圖2)。

2 炸油燒熱，中火將土司鑲肉(肉面朝下)炸約2分鐘至熟，撈出切三角形狀即成。可與「涼拌甜黃瓜」(見11頁)食用。

1 Stir 1 and 2 until sticky (use food processor or hands). Spread over bread (Fig.2, P.32).

2 Heat oil for deep-frying then fry bread (meat facing down)in medium heat 2 minutes until toasted. Remove and cut toast into triangular shapes. May be served with "sweet cucumber sauce" (P.11).

香炸雞蛋
Son in Law Eggs

<table>
<tr><td></td><td>熟蛋(去殼) ……………… 4個</td></tr>
<tr><td rowspan="2">1</td><td>蒜(切片) ………………… 8瓣</td></tr>
<tr><td>洋葱(切絲) ……………… ½個</td></tr>
<tr><td></td><td>炸油……………………… 適量</td></tr>
<tr><td></td><td>芫荽 ……………………… 適量</td></tr>
</table>

<table>
<tr><td></td><td>4 hard boiled eggs, shelled</td></tr>
<tr><td rowspan="2">1</td><td>8 garlic cloves, sliced</td></tr>
<tr><td>½ shredded onion</td></tr>
<tr><td></td><td>oil for deep-frying
cilantro as desired</td></tr>
</table>

1 炸油燒熱，中火將蛋炸呈金黃色，撈出後切半。

2 油3大匙燒熱，炒香1料，鏟出後置於紙巾上吸油；將「海鮮沾料」(見10頁)澆在蛋上，上撒炒好的1料及芫荽即可。

1 Heat oil for deep-frying then deep-fry egg until golden. Remove and cut each egg in half.

2 Heat 3 T. oil then stir-fry 1 until fragrant. Remove and place on paper towel to absorb oil. Pour "tamarind sauce" (P.10) over eggs. Sprinkle with 1 and cilantro. Serve.

蟹盒
Dear Crab (Poo Cha)

1 蟹肉、蝦泥‥‥‥‥‥各¼杯
　 豬絞肉‥‥‥‥‥‥‥‥ 4兩

2 魚露‥‥‥‥‥‥‥‥‥ 1大匙
　 胡椒‥‥‥‥‥‥‥‥‥¼小匙
　 糖‥‥‥‥‥‥‥‥‥‥½小匙
　 蒜、芫荽莖(切碎)‥‥各1大匙

　 蛋‥‥‥‥‥‥‥‥‥‥ 3個
　 蟹殼‥‥‥‥‥‥‥‥‥ 2個
　 炸油‥‥‥‥‥‥‥‥‥‥適量

1 ¼ c. ea: snow crab meat,
　 ground shrimp
　 ⅓ 1b. (150g) ground pork

2 1 T. fish sauce
　 ¼ t. pepper
　 ½ t. sugar
　 1 T. ea (minced): garlic,
　 cilantro roots

3 eggs
2 crab shells
oil for deep-frying

1 將①、②料及1個蛋用攪拌機或用手攪拌至有粘性，放入蟹殼內(圖1)。

2 蒸鍋內加水燒開，將蟹盒蒸15分鐘取出。

3 炸油燒熱，2個蛋打勻，蟹盒沾蛋液以中火炸呈金黃色(約3分鐘)撈出，可與「涼拌黃瓜」(見11頁)配食。

1 Mix ①, ②, and 1 egg thoroughly until sticky (by food processor or hand). Distribute mixture into crab shells (Fig. 1).

2 Bring water to boil then steam shells 15 minutes; remove.

3 Heat oil for deep-frying. Beat 2 eggs. Dip crab filled shells in eggs then deep-fry in medium heat 3 minutes until golden. May be served with "cucumber sauce" (P.11).

Fig. 1

蛋包什錦
Thai Stuffed Omelet

絞肉（豬、牛或雞肉）…… 3兩
蒜末……………………½小匙

|1| 洋葱丁、紅蘿蔔丁 … 各1大匙
芹菜丁 ……………… 2大匙
青豆仁 ……………… 1大匙
小番茄（切半）………… 3粒
草菇（罐頭）…………… 6個

|2| 魚露………………………¾大匙
鮮味露（圖1）、糖……各1小匙
番茄調味汁 …………… 1大匙

蛋（打散）………………… 2個

1 油2大匙燒熱，炒香蒜末，隨入肉炒熟，依序入 1 、 2 料拌炒後即鏟出。

2 在乾淨鍋面塗少許油，用中火將蛋液煎成蛋皮。

3 將炒好材料置蛋皮上，對摺成半圓形即成。

¼ 1b. (115g) ground pork,
   beef, or chicken
½ t. minced garlic

|1|
1 T. chopped onion
1 T. chopped carrot
2 T. chopped celery
1 T. green peas
3 cherry tomatoes, cut in
   half
6 canned straw mushrooms

|2|
¾ T. fish sauce
1 t. maggi sauce (Fig.1)
1 t. sugar
1 T. tomato sauce

2 beaten eggs

1 Heat 2 T. oil then stir-fry garlic until fragrant. Add meat and stir-fry until color changes. Add 1 then 2 ; stir to mix. Remove.

2 Lightly oil a clean pan. Fry eggs in medium heat to form a pancake.

3 Place stir-fried mixture over egg pancake then fold it over in half; serve.

Fig. 1

淡菜煎
Fried Mussels

淡菜（圖1）···················· 12個

① 番茄醬 ····················· 1大匙
辣椒醬（圖2）·············· 1小匙
醋 ···························· 2大匙
糖、水 ·················· 各4大匙
塩 ··························· ¼小匙

蒜末 ························· 1小匙

② 乾澄粉（圖3）··············3大匙
太白粉 ····················· 2大匙
水 ···························· 8大匙
塩 ··························· ⅛小匙

③ 蛋（打散）·················· 2個
葱花、芫荽 ··········· 各2大匙
豆芽·························· ½杯

12 mussels (Fig.1)

① 1 T. ketchup
1 t. chili paste (Fig.2)
2 T. vinegar
4 T. ea: sugar, water
¼ t. salt

1 t. minced garlic

② 3 T. tapioca starch (Fig.3)
2 T. cornstarch
8 T. water, ⅛ t. salt

③ 2 beaten eggs
2 T. ea (chopped): green
onion, cilantro
½ c. bean sprouts

Fig. 1

Fig. 2

Fig. 3

1 淡菜洗淨，入滾水內煮至開口即撈出，取出貝肉。①料煮開成沾料。

2 油2大匙燒熱，炒香蒜，先入貝肉爆香，再將調勻的②料炒至略凝固，再入③料略炒後壓平，二面略煎與沾料或「辣椒魚露」（見11頁）食用。

● 淡菜可用生蠔取代。

● 如無乾澄粉可用蕃薯粉、麵粉、玉米粉或其他粉取代。

1 Rinse mussels then cook in boiling water until they open. Remove mussel meat. Bring ① to boil to make dipping sauce.

2 Heat 2 T. oil then stir-fry garlic until fragrant. Add mussel meat and stir-fry until fragrant. Add mixture ② and quickly stir until mixture solidifies slightly (do not overcook). Add ③ and stir-fry briefly then lightly flatten to form a big pancake. Fry both sides of the pancake briefly. Serve with dipping sauce or "chili fish sauce" (P.11).

● Oysters may be substituted for mussels.

● If tapioca starch is not available, substitute with sweet potato powder, flour, or cornstarch.

炸全魚
Fried Cat Fish

魚 1 條 ⋯⋯⋯⋯⋯⋯⋯ 1斤

1 | 薑末 ⋯⋯⋯⋯⋯⋯⋯ 2大匙
蒜粉(圖1)⋯⋯⋯⋯⋯ 2大匙

2 | 太白粉、麵粉⋯⋯⋯ 各½杯
塩、胡椒 ⋯⋯⋯⋯⋯ 各2小匙

炸油⋯⋯⋯⋯⋯⋯⋯⋯ 適量

1⅓ 1b. (600g) whole fish

1 | 2 T. minced ginger
2 T. garlic powder (Fig.1)

2 | ½ c. ea: cornstarch, flour
2 t. ea: salt, pepper

oil for deep-frying

1 魚洗淨,拭乾水份,魚身兩面斜切,刀深觸及大骨,用 1 料擦勻魚身,切縫均需擦勻,並將 2 料仔細沾裹縛緊魚身。若不馬上炸,須將魚以在水中游水的姿式,備好在盤內,以免切口合上。

2 炸油燒熱,提起魚尾,順著魚在水中游水的姿式投入油鍋,用鍋鏟淋熱油於魚身,使魚身花紋定型,並以大火炸約10分鐘至魚肉熟外皮脆即撈出,沾「辣椒魚露」(見11頁)食用。

1 Rinse fish and pat dry. Hold a cutting knife so the blade is at a 30° angle. Make diagonal cuts through the meat to the bone every 1″(2cm) on both sides of the fish. Rub fish and inside cuts with mixture 1. Coat fish completely and place belly down to keep cuts in an "open" position.

2 Heat oil for deep-frying. Carefully lift fish by the tail and gently lower into wok. Ladle some hot oil over the fish. Fry fish over high heat 10 minutes, or until the fish is cooked and the skin has become crispy. Serve with "chili fish sauce" (P.11).

Fig. 1

什錦魚
Fried Pompano with Sweet & Sour Sauce

鯧魚1條(圖1)⋯⋯⋯⋯⋯⋯⋯12兩
蒜末⋯⋯⋯⋯⋯⋯⋯⋯⋯⋯½小匙

1 洋葱、紅椒、青椒、
　　番茄、黃瓜、鳳梨、
　　紅蘿蔔、薑絲 ⋯⋯⋯⋯ 共2杯

2 魚露 ⋯⋯⋯⋯⋯⋯⋯⋯ 1¾大匙
　　糖、醋 ⋯⋯⋯⋯⋯⋯ 各1½大匙

3 高湯(或水) ⋯⋯⋯⋯⋯ 4大匙
　　太白粉 ⋯⋯⋯⋯⋯⋯⋯ 1小匙

炸油⋯⋯⋯⋯⋯⋯⋯⋯⋯⋯⋯適量

**1 1b. (450g) whole fish
(Fig.1)**
½ t. minced garlic

1 **total of 2 c.: onion, red and
green bell peppers,
tomato, cucumber,
pineapple, carrot,
shredded ginger**

2 **1¾ T. fish sauce
1½ T. ea: sugar, vinegar**

3 **4 T. stock or water
1 t. cornstarch**

oil for deep-frying

1 魚洗淨拭乾水份，魚身兩面各劃3刀。

2 炸油燒熱，放入魚以大火炸約6分鐘至酥脆，即撈出。

3 油2大匙燒熱，炒香蒜，依序入 **1** 、 **2** 料拌炒後，再加調勻的 **3** 料勾汁，澆在炸好的魚上即成。

1 Rinse fish and pat dry; cut 3 lines vertically on both sides of fish.

2 Heat oil for deep-frying then fry fish in high heat 6 minutes until crispy; remove.

3 Heat 2 T. oil then stir-fry garlic until fragrant. Add ☐1 then ☐2; stir-fry to mix well. Thicken with mixture ☐3. Pour over fish; serve.

Fig. 1

甜味炒雞肉
Stir-fried Sweet Chicken

雞肉（切條）……………… 8兩

① 白醬油、酒、太白粉 各1小匙

② 蒜末 ……………………… 1小匙
辣椒膏（圖1）…………… 1大匙

③ 魚露 …………………… 1½大匙
甜醬油 ………………… 1½小匙
糖 ……………………… ½小匙

高湯（或水）…………… 2大匙
腰果 …………………………… ¼杯

⅔ 1b. (300g) boneless
chicken, cut in strips

① 1 t. ea: thin soy sauce,
cooking wine, cornstarch

② 1 t. minced garlic
1 T. chili paste with soya
bean oil (Fig.1)

③ 1½ T. fish sauce
1½ t. sweet soy sauce
½ t. sugar

2 T. stock or water
¼ c. cashew nuts

1 雞肉拌入①料略醃。

2 油2大匙燒熱，炒香②料，隨入雞肉炒熟，續入③料拌炒後，再加高湯、腰果燒開即成。

● 如無辣椒膏時，可用沙茶醬來取代。

1 Marinate chicken with ①.

2 Heat 2 T. oil then stir-fry ② until fragrant. Add chicken and stir-fry until cooked. Add ③ and stir to mix. Add stock and cashew nuts then bring to boil; serve.

● Barbecue (Sa Tsa) sauce may be used for "chili paste with soya bean oil".

Fig. 1

辣味炒雞肉
Stir-fried Spicy Chicken & Cashew Nuts

雞肉（切條）⋯⋯⋯⋯⋯ 6兩

1
蒜末 ⋯⋯⋯⋯⋯⋯⋯ 1小匙
乾辣椒 ⋯⋯⋯⋯⋯⋯ 6條
大乾辣椒（切塊）⋯⋯⋯ 1條

2 洋蔥塊、腰果 ⋯⋯⋯ 共2杯

3
魚露 ⋯⋯⋯⋯⋯⋯⋯ 1½大匙
甜醬油 ⋯⋯⋯⋯⋯⋯ 1½小匙
糖 ⋯⋯⋯⋯⋯⋯⋯⋯ ½小匙

4
蔥段 ⋯⋯⋯⋯⋯⋯⋯ ¼杯
高湯（或水）⋯⋯⋯⋯ 2大匙

½ 1b. (225g) boneless
chicken, cut in strips

1
1 t. minced garlic
6 dried chilies
1 dried New Mexico chili,
cut in pieces

2 total of 2 c.: onion chunks,
cashew nuts

3
1½ T. fish sauce
1½ t. sweet soy sauce
½ t. sugar

4
¼ c. green onion sections
2 T. stock or water

1 油2大匙燒熱，炒香 1 料，隨入肉炒熟，依序入 2 、 3 料拌炒後，再加 4 料，燒開即成。

● 1 料見圖1。如無乾辣椒時，可用新鮮辣椒或辣椒醬等來應用。

● 甜醬油的作用是加深菜餚的顏色。

1 Heat 2 T. oil then stir-fry 1 until fragrant. Add meat and stir-fry until color changes. Add 2 then 3 ; stir-fry briefly. Add 4 and bring to boil. Serve.

● See Fig.1 for 1 . Fresh chili or chili paste may be used in place of dried chili.

● Sweet soy sauce (caramel) is used to enhance the color of a dish.

Fig. 1

薑炒雞肉
Ginger Chicken

雞肉（切條）⋯⋯⋯⋯⋯⋯ 6兩

1 | 薑絲⋯⋯⋯⋯⋯⋯⋯⋯¼杯
豆瓣醬（圖1）、蒜末⋯各1小匙

2 | 洋葱、乾木耳（泡軟）切條共2杯

3 | 魚露⋯⋯⋯⋯⋯⋯⋯1½大匙
甜醬油⋯⋯⋯⋯⋯⋯1½小匙
糖⋯⋯⋯⋯⋯⋯⋯⋯⋯½小匙

4 | 葱段⋯⋯⋯⋯⋯⋯⋯⋯¼杯
高湯（或水）⋯⋯⋯⋯⋯2大匙

½ 1b. (225g) boneless
  chicken, cut in strips

1 | ¼ c. shredded ginger
1 t. ea: soy bean condiment
  (Fig.1), minced garlic

2 | total of 2 c. (stripped):
  onion, dried wood ears
  (pre-softened in cold water)

3 | 1½ T. fish sauce
1½ t. sweet soy sauce
½ t. sugar

4 | ¼ c. green onions,
  cut 1″ (2cm) long
2 T. stock or water

1 油2大匙燒熱，炒香1料，隨入肉炒熟，依序入2、3料拌炒後，再加4料燒開即成。

● 2料見圖2。

1 Heat 2 T. oil then stir-fry 1 until fragrant. Add meat and stir-fry until color changes. Add 2 then 3; stir to mix. Add 4 and bring to boil. Serve.

● See Fig.2 for 2.

Fig. 1

Fig. 2

蒜炒雞肉
Spicy Garlic Chicken

雞肉（切條） …………… 8兩

① 白醬油、酒、太白粉 各1小匙

② 蒜、芫荽莖（切碎）… 各1大匙

③ 魚露 ………………… 1½大匙
甜醬油 ……………… 1½小匙
糖 ……………………½小匙
胡椒 ………………… 1小匙

高湯（或水）………… 2大匙

²⁄₃ 1b. (300g) boneless
chicken, cut in strips

① 1 t. ea: thin soy sauce,
cooking wine, cornstarch

② 1 T. ea (minced): garlic,
cilantro roots

③ 1½ T. fish sauce
1½ t. sweet soy sauce
½ t. sugar
1 t. pepper

2 T. stock or water

1 雞肉拌入①料略醃。

2 油2大匙燒熱炒香②料，隨入肉炒熟，加③料拌炒後，再加高湯燒開即成。

● 忙碌者可將多量肉切好，拌入醃料，分裝冷凍保存；每次取一份解凍，並加太白粉拌匀後使用。

1 Marinate chicken in ①.

2 Heat 2 T. oil then stir-fry ② until fragrant. Add meat and stir-fry until color changes. Add ③ then stir to mix. Add stock and bring to boil. Serve.

● To save time, large quantities of meat may be cut, marinated, frozen, and stored in several small bags for later use. Defrost one bag of meat for each use; mix meat with cornstarch. Combine with 1 T. oil before frying.

筍片炒雞肉
Chili Chicken & Bamboo Shoots

雞肉(切條) ⋯⋯⋯⋯⋯⋯⋯ 6兩
蒜末⋯⋯⋯⋯⋯⋯⋯⋯⋯½小匙

1 | 筍片(罐頭)、薄荷葉 ⋯ 共2杯

2 | 魚露 ⋯⋯⋯⋯⋯⋯⋯⋯ 1½大匙
| 糖⋯⋯⋯⋯⋯⋯⋯⋯⋯½小匙
| 辣椒醬 ⋯⋯⋯⋯⋯⋯ 1½小匙

椰奶 ⋯⋯⋯⋯⋯⋯⋯⋯⋯ 4大匙

½ 1b. (225g) boneless
  chicken, cut in strips
½ t. minced garlic

1 | total of 2 c.: canned
  bamboo shoots, mint
  leaves

2 | 1½ T. fish sauce
  ½ t. sugar
  1½ t. chili paste

4 T. coconut milk

1 油2大匙燒熱，炒香蒜，隨入肉炒熟，依序入1、2料拌炒後再加椰奶燒開即成。

● 1料見圖1。如能使用新鮮筍，炒出來的菜餚味道更佳。

1 Heat 2 T. oil then stir-fry garlic until fragrant. Add meat and stir-fry until color changes. Add 1 then 2; stir to mix.
Add coconut milk and bring to boil. Serve.

● See Fig. 1 for 1. Use fresh bamboo shoots, if possible, to enhance flavor.

Fig. 1

43

玉米筍炒雞肉
Chicken & Baby Corn

雞肉（切條）……………… 6兩
蒜末………………………½小匙

1 | 玉米筍、草菇（罐頭）… 共2杯

2 | 魚露、蠔油…………各¾大匙
甜醬油、醋 ………… 各1小匙
糖…………………………½小匙

3 | 葱段、高湯（或水）……各¼杯
太白粉 …………………… 1小匙

½ 1b. (225g) boneless
chicken, cut in strips
½ t. minced garlic

1 | total of 2 c. (canned): baby
corn, straw mushrooms

2 | ¾ T. fish sauce
¾ T. oyster sauce
1 t. sweet soy sauce
1 t. vinegar
½ t. sugar

3 | ¼ c. green onions,
cut 1″ (2cm) long
¼ c. stock or water
1 t. cornstarch

1 油2大匙燒熱，炒香蒜，隨入肉炒熟，依序入 1 、 2 料拌炒後再加調勻的 3 料勾汁即成。

● 1 料見圖1。可用毛菇或香菇等取代草菇。

1 Heat 2 T. oil then stir-fry garlic until fragrant. Add meat and stir-fry until color changes. Add 1 then 2 ; stir to mix. Add mixture 3 to thicken. Serve.

● See Fig. 1 for 1 . Button mushrooms or Chinese black mushrooms may be used for straw mushrooms.

Fig. 1

Fig. 2

Fig. 3

豆芽炒肉片
Pork & Bean Sprouts

猪肉（切片）……………………4兩
蒜末……………………………½小匙

1 鹹酸菜（切塊）
　豆腐干（切片）……… 共1½杯

2 豆芽、葱段……………… 共1½杯

3 魚露……………………………1大匙
　糖………………………………½小匙

⅓ lb. (150g) sliced pork
½ t. minced garlic

1 total of 1½ c.: salty mustard
　greens pieces, pressed
　bean curd slices

2 total of 1½ c.: bean sprouts;
　green onion sections

3 1 T. fish sauce
　½ t. sugar

1 油2大匙燒熱，炒香蒜，隨入肉炒熟，依序入 1、2、3料拌炒均匀即成。

● 1料見44頁，圖2。鹹酸菜是大芥菜以鹽醃漬製成，沖水後使用；豆腐乾是豆腐脫水後製成。

1 Heat 2 T. oil then stir-fry garlic until fragrant. Add meat and stir-fry until color changes. Add 1, 2, then 3; stir to mix. Serve.

● See Fig. 2, P. 44 for 1. Salty mustard greens are made by allowing mustard greens, marinated in salt, to ferment; rinse with fresh water before using. Pressed bean curd is made by flattening bean curd to squeeze out the liquid.

咖哩炒肉
Stir-fried Pork & Curry
(Prik King Pork)

猪肉（切片）………………… 8兩
紅咖哩醬………………………1大匙
四季豆（切段、見44頁，圖3）3大匙

1 魚露……………………………1大匙
　糖………………………………2小匙
　紅椒粉…………………………½小匙
　蝦粉（見9頁）…………………1小匙

　高湯（或水）………………… 2大匙

1 油3大匙以中火炒香紅咖哩醬，隨入肉炒熟，依序入四季豆及 1料拌炒後，再加高湯燒開即成。

● 可用雞肉或蝦來取代豬肉。

⅔ lb. (300g) sliced pork
1 T. red curry paste
3 T. string beans, cut
　2˝ (5cm) long (Fig.3, P.44)

1 1 T. fish sauce，2 t. sugar
　½ t. paprika powder
　1 t. dried shrimp powder
　(P.9)

2 T. stock or water

1 Heat 3 T. oil then stir-fry curry paste until fragrant. Add meat and stir-fry until color changes. Add string beans then 1; stir to mix. Add stock and bring to boil. Serve.

● Chicken or shrimp may be substituted for pork.

蠔油炒牛肉
Stir-fried Beef & Oyster Sauce

牛肉(切片) ················· 6兩

[1] 白醬油、酒、太白粉 各1小匙

蒜末 ······················· ½小匙

[2] 洋葱、紅椒
青椒、草菇 ········ 切塊共2杯

[3] 白醬油、蠔油········ 各¾大匙
甜醬油 ···················· 1小匙

[4] 葱段、高湯(或水)······各¼杯
太白粉 ···················· 1小匙

½ 1b. (225g) beef, sliced

[1] 1 t. ea: thin soy sauce,
cooking wine, cornstarch

½ t. minced garlic

[2] total of 2 c. (cut in pieces):
onion, red bell pepper,
green bell pepper, straw
mushrooms

[3] ¾ T. ea: thin soy sauce,
oyster sauce
1 t. sweet soy sauce

[4] ¼ c. green onions,
cut 1″ (2cm) long
¼ c. stock or water
1 t. cornstarch

1 牛肉拌入[1]料略醃。

2 油2大匙燒熱,炒香蒜,隨入牛肉略炒,依序入[2]、[3]料拌炒後,再加調勻的[4]料勾汁即成。

● [2]料見圖1。

1 Marinate beef with [1].

2 Heat 2 T. oil then stir-fry garlic until fragrant. Add beef and stir-fry briefly. Add [2] then [3]; stir to mix. Thicken with mixture [4]. Serve.

● See Fig. 1 for [2].

Fig. 1

糖醋炒肉
Sweet & Sour Pork

豬肉(切片) ················ 6兩
蒜末 ······················· ½小匙

1 洋葱、青椒、黃瓜、芹菜、
小番茄、鳳梨···· 切塊共2杯

2 魚露 ···················· 1½大匙
糖、醋、番茄醬 ····· 各1大匙

3 高湯(或水) ············· 4大匙
太白粉 ·················· 1小匙

½ lb. (225g) sliced pork
½ t. minced garlic

1 total of 2 c. (cut in pieces):
onion, green bell pepper,
cucumber, celery, cherry
tomato, pineapple

2 1½ T. fish sauce
1 T. ea: sugar, vinegar,
ketchup

3 4 T. stock or water
1 t. cornstarch

1 油2大匙燒熱，炒香蒜，隨入肉炒熟，依序入 1 、 2 料拌炒後，再加調勻的
3 料勾汁即成。

1 Heat 2 T. oil then stir-fry garlic until fragrant. Add meat and stir-fry
until color changes. Add 1 then 2 ; stir to mix. Add mixture 3 to
thicken. Serve.

茄子炒絞肉
Fried Eggplant & Ground Pork

豬絞肉 ······················ 6兩
茄子(切塊) ················ 2杯

1 | 蒜末、辣椒末 ········ 各1小匙
豆瓣醬(圖1) ············ 1小匙

2 | 魚露、白醬油 ········ 各¾大匙
糖、甜醬油 ·········· 各½小匙

3 | 九層塔 ····················· 20片
高湯(或水) ··········· 3大匙

½ lb. (225g) ground pork
2 c. eggplant, cut in pieces

1 | 1 t. ea (minced): garlic, chili
1 t. soy bean condiment
(Fig.1)

2 | ¾ T. fish sauce
¾ T. thin soy sauce
½ t. sugar
½ t. sweet soy sauce

3 | 20 basil leaves
3 T. stock or water

1 茄子在滾水內燙約30秒，即撈出。

2 油2大匙燒熱，炒香1料，隨入肉炒熟，依序入茄子及2料拌炒後，再加3料燒開即成。

● 此道菜內茄子煮出來是脆的，如喜食軟茄子者，燙煮時間需加長。

1 Cook eggplant in boiling water 30 seconds; remove.

2 Heat 2 T. oil then stir-fry ① until fragrant. Add meat and stir-fry until color changes. Add eggplant then ②; stir to mix. Add ③ bring to boil. Serve

● The cooked eggplant in this dish is crispy. If soft eggplant is preferred, increase cooking time.

Fig. 1

Fig. 2

蒜炒蝦
Spicy Garlic Shrimp

蝦（無殼）· · · · · · · · · · · · · · · 8兩

1 蒜、芫荽莖（切碎）· · · 各1大匙
   胡椒 · · · · · · · · · · · · · · · · · · · 1小匙

2 魚露、鮮味露 · · · · · · · 各¾大匙
   糖 · ½小匙

高湯（或水）· · · · · · · · · · · · 2大匙

⅔ lb. (300g) shelled shrimp

1 1 T. ea (minced): garlic,
   cilantro roots
   1 t. pepper

2 ¾ T. fish sauce
   ¾ T. maggi sauce
   ½ t. sugar

2 T. stock or water

---

1 蝦抽去腸泥，洗淨後瀝乾水份。

2 油2大匙與奶油1大匙燒熱，炒香1料，隨入蝦炒熟，續入2料拌炒後，再加高湯燒開即成。

1 Devein shrimp; rinse and drain.

2 Heat 2 T. oil and 1 T. butter; stir-fry 1 until fragrant. Add shrimp and stir-fry until color changes. Add 2 and stir to mix. Add stock and bring to boil. Serve.

粉絲炒蝦
Shrimp & Sliver Noodles

蝦（無殼）· · · · · · · · · · · · · · · 4兩

1 大蝦膏（見86頁，圖1）1½大匙
   蒜末 · · · · · · · · · · · · · · · · · · · 1小匙

2 乾粉絲（泡軟、見48頁，圖2）⅔兩
   洋葱（切塊）· · · · · · · · · · · · ¼個
   草菇（罐頭）· · · · · · · · · · · · 8個

3 魚露 · · · · · · · · · · · · · · · · 1½大匙
   糖 · ½小匙

4 葱段 · · · · · · · · · · · · · · · · · · · ¼杯
   高湯（或水）· · · · · · · · · · · · ½杯

⅓ lb. (150g) shelled shrimp

1 1½ T. shrimp paste with soya
   bean oil (Fig.1, P.86)
   1 t. minced garlic

2 1 oz. (28g) bean threads,
   softened in cold water
   (Fig.2, P.48)
   ¼ onion, cut in pieces
   8 canned straw mushrooms

3 1½ T. fish sauce
   ½ t. sugar

4 ¼ c. green onions,
   cut 1″ (2cm) long
   ½ c. stock or water

---

1 蝦抽去腸泥，洗淨後瀝乾水份。

2 油2大匙，炒香1料，隨入蝦炒熟，依序入2、3料拌炒後，再加4料燒開即成。

1 Devein shrimp; rinse and drain.

2 Heat 2 T. oil then stir-fry 1 until fragrant. Add shrimp and stir-fry until color changes. Add 2 then 3; stir to mix. Add 4 and bring to boil. Serve.

咖哩炒蝦
Sauteed Shrimp in Curry Sauce

1
- 蝦（無殼）⋯⋯⋯⋯⋯⋯ 4兩
- 冷凍蟹鉗 ⋯⋯⋯⋯⋯⋯ 4個

2
- 蒜末 ⋯⋯⋯⋯⋯⋯⋯⋯ 1小匙
- 辣椒粉、咖哩粉⋯⋯ 各½小匙

3
- 洋葱、芹菜、紅椒、青椒⋯共2杯

4
- 魚露 ⋯⋯⋯⋯⋯⋯⋯ 1½大匙
- 糖⋯⋯⋯⋯⋯⋯⋯⋯⋯ ½小匙

5
- 葱段⋯⋯⋯⋯⋯⋯⋯⋯ ¼杯
- 高湯（或水）⋯⋯⋯⋯ 2大匙

1
- ⅓ lb. (150g) shelled shrimp
- 4 frozen crab claws

2
- 1 t. minced garlic
- ½ t. ea: ground chili, curry powder

3
- total of 2 c. (stripped): onion, celery, red and green bell peppers

4
- 1½ T. fish sauce
- ½ t. sugar

5
- ¼ c. green onion, cut 1" (2cm) long
- 2 T. stock or water

1 蝦抽去腸泥，洗淨後瀝乾水份，蟹鉗解凍後備用。

2 油2大匙燒熱，炒香②料，隨入①料炒熟，依序入③、④料拌炒後，再加⑤料燒開即成。

● ③料見圖1。

1 Devein shrimp; rinse and drain. Defrost crab claws and set aside.

2 Heat 2 T. oil then stir-fry ② until fragrant. Add ① and stir-fry until color changes. Add ③ then ④; stir to mix. Add ⑤ and bring to boil. Serve.

● See Fig. 1 for ③.

Fig. 1

Fig. 2

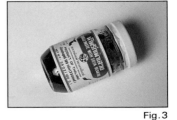

Fig. 3

辣椒炒魷魚
Stir-fried Chili Squid

魷魚	……………………	8兩
1	蒜末 ……………………	1小匙
	辣椒（切絲）……………	6條
2	魚露 ……………………	1½大匙
	甜醬油 …………………	1½小匙
	糖 ………………………	½小匙
3	九層塔 …………………	20片
	高湯（或水）……………	2大匙

⅔ lb. (300g) squid

1
1 t. minced garlic
6 shredded chilies

2
1½ T. fish sauce
1½ t. sweet soy sauce
½ t. sugar

3
20 basil leaves
2 T. stock or water

1 魷魚去除薄膜，洗淨後在內面劃交叉刀痕並切塊（見50頁，圖2）。

2 油2大匙燒熱，炒香 **1** 料，隨入魷魚炒至捲起，續入 **2** 料拌炒後，再加 **3** 料燒開即成。

1 Prepare squid and score inside surfaces; then cut squid in pieces (Fig.2, P.50).

2 Heat 2 T. oil then stir-fry **1** until fragrant. Add squid and stirfry until curled. Add **2** then stir to mix. Add **3** and bring to boil. Serve.

辣椒炒蛤蜊
Rock & Roll Clams

蛤蜊	…………………	12兩
1	蒜末 ……………………	1小匙
	辣椒（切絲）……………	6條
	辣椒膏（見50頁，圖3）…	1大匙
2	魚露 ……………………	1½大匙
	糖 ………………………	½小匙
3	薄荷葉 …………………	30片
	高湯（或水）……………	4大匙

1 lb. (450g) clams

1
1 t. minced garlic
6 shredded chilies
1 T. chili paste with soya bean oil (Fig.3, P.50)

2
1½ T. fish sauce
½ t. sugar

3
30 mint leaves
4 T. stock or water

1 油2大匙燒熱，炒香 **1** 料，依序入蛤蜊及 **2** 料拌炒後再加 **3** 料蓋鍋煮至蛤蜊開口即成。

● 無如辣椒膏時，可用沙茶醬取代。

1 Heat 2 T. oil then stir-fry **1** until fragrant. Add clams then **2**; stir to mix. Add **3** then cover; cook until clams open.

● If chili paste is not available, B.B.Q. sauce (Sa Tsa) may be used.

黃瓜炒蛋
Sauteed Cucumber & Egg

蝦（無殼）· · · · · · · · · · · · · · · · 4兩
蛋 · 1個
蒜末 · · · · · · · · · · · · · · · · · · · ½小匙

☐1 黃瓜、青椒、紅椒 ··· 切條共2杯
乾木耳（泡軟）

☐2 魚露 · · · · · · · · · · · · · · · · · 1大匙
白醬油 · · · · · · · · · · · · · · · ½大匙
胡椒 · · · · · · · · · · · · · · · · · ¼小匙
糖 · · · · · · · · · · · · · · · · · · · ½小匙

高湯（或水）· · · · · · · · · · · 2大匙

⅓ 1b. (150g) shelled shrimp
1 egg
½ t. minced garlic

☐1 total of 2 c. (stripped):
cucumber, green & red
bell pepper, dried wood
ears softened in cold water

☐2 1 T. fish sauce
½ T. thin soy sauce
¼ t. pepper
½ t. sugar

2 T. stock or water

1 蝦抽去腸泥，洗淨後瀝乾水份。

2 油2大匙燒熱，炒香蒜，隨入蝦炒熟，依序入蛋及☐1、☐2料拌炒後再加高湯燒開即成。

● ☐1料見圖1。

1 Devein shrimp; rinse and drain.

2 Heat 2 T. oil then stir-fry garlic until fragrant. Add shrimp and stir-fry until color changes. Add egg, ☐1, then ☐2; stir to mix. Add stock and bring to boil. Serve.

● See Fig. 1 for ☐1

Fig. 1

Fig. 2

Fig. 3

紅燒玉桂鴨
Cinnamon Duck

鴨半隻 ················· 約1斤	

1
椰子糖 ················· 1大匙
五香粉（見52頁，圖2）··· 2小匙
胡椒 ·················· ½小匙
蒜、芫荽莖（切碎）··· 各1大匙

2
水 ···················· 3杯
白醬油 ··············· 2½大匙
甜醬油 ················ 1小匙
玉桂（見52頁，圖3）····· ½根

½ duck, 1⅓ lb. (600g)

1
- 1 T. palm sugar
- 2 t. palo powder or five spice powder (Fig.2, P.52)
- ½ t. pepper
- 1 T. ea (minced): garlic, cilantro roots

2
- 3 c. water
- 2½ T. thin soy sauce
- 1 t. sweet soy sauce
- ½ cinnamon stick (Fig.3, P.52)

1 油1大匙炒香①料，隨入鴨及②料燒開，改中火蓋鍋（煮時需翻轉）煮約1小時至肉軟，汁略收乾。待涼後去骨切塊，沾「烤肉沾料」（見11頁）食用。

1 Heat 1 T. oil then stir-fry ① until fragrant. Add duck and ②; bring to boil. Reduce heat to medium; cover and cook 1 hour until meat is tender and liquid is slightly evaporated (turn duck over several times during cooking). Let stand to cool; remove bones and cut duck in pieces. Serve with "Thai B.B.Q sauce" (P.11).

紅燒肉
Pork Cooked in Soy Sauce
(Pork Pa-Lo)

豬肉（切塊）·············· 8兩	
蛋（煮熟去殼）············ 2個	

1
①料同上

2
水 ···················· 1杯
白醬油 ··············· 2½大匙
甜醬油 ················ 1小匙
玉桂 ·················· ½根

⅔ lb. (300g) pork, cut in pieces
2 hard boiled eggs, shelled

1
- see ① in above recipe

2
- 1 c. water
- 2½ T. thin soy sauce
- 1 t. sweet soy sauce
- ½ cinnamon stick

1 油1大匙燒熱，炒香①料，隨入豬肉、蛋及②料燒開，改中火蓋鍋煮約30分鐘即成。

● 適合煮一大鍋，分數次食用。

1 Heat 1 T. oil then stir-fry ① until fragrant. Add pork, eggs, and ②; bring to boil. Cover and cook over medium heat 30 minutes until meat is tender.

● Large quantities may be cooked for several serving times.

什錦菜鍋
Assorted Vegetable Soup (Tom Chab Chai)

1 蒜末、辣椒末 ········ 各1小匙
　豆瓣醬、糖 ········ 各½大匙

2 魚露、白醬油 ········ 各1大匙
　水 ················ 2½杯
　豬排骨(切塊，圖1) ········ 6兩

3 白蘿蔔、大白菜
　芹菜、豆腐 ··· 切塊共3杯

4 乾粉絲(泡軟) ········ ⅔兩
　乾木耳(泡軟) ········ ¼杯
　毛菇 ················ 4個

1 1 t. ea (minced): garlic, chili
　½ T. soy bean condiment
　½ T. sugar

2 1 T. fish sauce
　1 T. thin soy sauce
　2½ c. water
　½ 1b. (225g) pork back
　　ribs, cut in pieces (Fig.1)

3 total of 3 c. (cut in pieces):
　white radish (dai kon),
　nappa cabbage, celery,
　bean curd (tofu)

4 1 oz. (28g) dried bean
　threads, softened in cold
　water
　¼ c. dried wood ears,
　softened in cold water
　4 mushrooms

1 油2大匙燒熱，炒香1料，放入2料燒開，去除白沫，入3料再燒開，改中火煮20分鐘，隨入4料煮開即成。

● 4料見圖2。此菜可多煮，分次食用。

1 Heat 2 T. oil then stir-fry 1 until fragrant. Add 2 and bring to boil. Remove scum. Add 3 and bring to boil. Cook 20 minutes in medium heat. Add 4 then bring to another boil. Serve.

● See Fig.2, for 4 . This dish may be prepared in large quantity and divided for several meals.

Fig. 1

Fig. 2

軟皮春捲
Steamed Eggrolls

春捲皮（圖1）⋯⋯⋯⋯⋯⋯⋯4片

1
白醬油、蘇梅醬（圖2）各2大匙
番茄醬 ⋯⋯⋯⋯⋯⋯⋯⋯⋯1大匙
糖 ⋯⋯⋯⋯⋯⋯⋯⋯⋯⋯⋯3大匙
醋 ⋯⋯⋯⋯⋯⋯⋯⋯⋯⋯⋯6大匙
太白粉⋯⋯⋯⋯⋯⋯⋯⋯⋯½小匙

蛋（打散）⋯⋯⋯⋯⋯⋯⋯⋯1個
中式香腸 ⋯⋯⋯⋯⋯⋯⋯⋯1條
蟹肉或假蟹肉 ⋯⋯⋯⋯⋯2兩
蝦（無殼）⋯⋯⋯⋯⋯⋯⋯2隻

2 豆芽、黃瓜絲、葱絲⋯各½杯

4 eggroll shells (Fig.1)

1
2 T. ea: thin soy sauce,
   plum sauce (Fig.2)
1 T. ketchup
3 T. sugar
6 T. vinegar
½ t. cornstarch

1 beaten egg
1 Chinese sausage
3 oz. (84g) crab meat
2 shelled shrimp

2
½ c. ea: green onion
   shreds, cucumber shreds,
   bean sprouts

1 將 **1** 料燒開即成沾料。

2 鍋燒熱，鍋面擦少許油，放入蛋液，煎成蛋皮後切絲。

3 香腸煮約4分鐘，切絲；蟹肉、蝦在滾水內煮至蝦變色撈出，蝦切半。

4 將蛋絲、香腸、蟹肉與 **2** 料放於春捲皮上，捲好共4條，置盤；蒸鍋內加水燒開，放入春捲蒸20秒取出；每條分切3小塊，蝦置春捲上，沾沾料食用。

1 Make dipping sauce by bringing **1** to boil.

2 Heat then grease pan. Fry egg to form a pancake then shred it.

3 Cook sausage 4 minutes then shred it. Cook crab meat and shrimp in boiling water until shrimp changes color; remove and cut shrimp in half.

4 Place egg shreds, sausage, crab meat, and **2** over eggroll shells. Roll up shell to make 4 rolls then place on a plate. Bring water to boil then steam rolls 20 seconds; remove. Cut each roll in 3 pieces. Place shrimp over eggroll. May be served with dipping sauce.

Fig. 1

Fig. 2

海鮮蒸蛋
Steamed Eggs & Seafood (Ho-Mok)

魚肉（切塊，圖1）…………2兩

1 陳皮、瑞中美（泡軟）… 各1大匙
　紅咖哩醬 … 2大匙、椰奶 … 1杯
　蛋……2個，糖、塩……各1大匙

2 波菜、九層塔、大白菜（切塊）共1杯

3 魚肉（切塊，圖1）…………2兩
　干貝………………………⅔兩
　蝦（無殼）………………2隻
　墨魚（切塊）……………⅔兩

椰奶漿……………………1大匙

4 芫荽、泰國檸檬葉…………適量
　紅辣椒絲…………………適量

3 oz. (84g) fish fillet, cut in pieces (Fig.1)

1　1 T. ea: kaffir skin, rhizome (softened in water)
　2 T. red curry paste
　1 c. coconut milk, 2 eggs
　1 T. ea: sugar, salt

2　Total of 1 c. (cut in pieces): spinach, nappa cabbage, basil leaves

3　3 oz. (84g) fish fillet, cut in pieces (Fig.1)
　1 oz. (28g) scallop
　2 shelled shrimp
　1 oz. (28g) squid, cut in pieces

1 T. thick coconut milk

4　cilantro, shredded kaffir leaves and red chili as desired

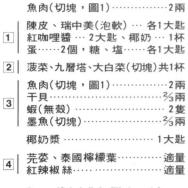

Fig. 1

Fig. 2

Fig. 3

1 蝦抽去腸泥，洗淨後瀝乾。魚肉與 1 料在果汁機內攪爛成蛋漿。

2 蒸碗內依序放入 2 、 3 料及蛋漿（約7分滿，避免蒸時溢出）；蒸鍋內加水燒開，放入準備好的蒸料小火蒸約20分鐘，即取出；淋上濃椰奶，撒上 4 料即成。

● 烤箱蒸法參照57頁。如用電鍋蒸，外鍋加水½杯，鍋蓋留一點縫，熄火後蓋緊再燜10分鐘即成。

● 1 料見圖2；陳皮與瑞中美是用來加強菜餚之香味。 2 料見圖3。

1 Devein shrimp; rinse and drain. Liquify fish and 1 in blender.

2 Put 2 , 3 , then fish and egg mixture in a steaming bowl (only fill to 70 % to prevent overflow during steaming). Bring water to boil; then reduce heat to low. Put in steaming bowl and steam the egg mixture 20 minutes. Pour on thick coconut milk then sprinkle with 4 . Serve.

● See P.57 for steaming by oven. If using rice cooker, put ½ c. water in cooker then steam the egg mixture with cover slightly open. After turning off, tightly close cooker cover 10 minutes. Serve.

● See Fig.2 for 1 ; kaffir skin and rhizome are used to enhance the flavor of the dish. See Fig. 3 for 2 .

絞肉蒸蛋
Steamed Eggs & ground pork (Kai Toon)

1
蛋（打散） ····················· 3個
豬絞肉 ························· 3兩
水 ·························· 1杯
葱花、白醬油 ········· 各2大匙
冬菜 ························· 1小匙
胡椒 ······················· ¼小匙

1
3 eggs, beaten
¼ 1b. (115g) ground pork
1 c. water
2 T. ea: chopped green
    onions, thin soy sauce
1 t. preserved cabbage
¼ t. pepper

1 蒸碗內放入拌勻的 1 料（約7分滿，避免蒸時溢出）。蒸鍋內加水燒開，放入
準備好的蒸料，小火蒸約20分鐘即成。

● 烤箱蒸法：將盛有 1 料的容器置烤盤內，放入熱水至半腰（不蓋），烤箱燒
至325˚F烤90分鐘。

● 蒸蛋的時間因所使用容器大小不同略有出入，蒸蛋時可隨時用叉子插入試
試，若無蛋液流出來即可。

1 Put mixture 1 in a steaming bowl (only fill to 70% to prevent
overflow during steaming). Bring water to boil, then reduce heat
to low. Put in steaming bowl and steam egg mixture 20 minutes.

● Steaming by oven : Preheat oven to 325˚F. Place the container
with 1 in a baking pan. Pour hot water in baking pan to half way
up the container (Do not cover). Put baking pan in oven and bake
90 minutes.

● Steaming time may vary due to the size of the container. Check
for doneness by inserting fork in egg. If the fork is clean when
removed, the egg is cooked.

蔬菜豬肉咖哩
Jungle Pork & Red Curry

豬肉(切塊) ················ 6兩

1
水 ···················· 1½杯
紅咖哩醬 ············· 1½大匙
泰式薑 ················ 2片
瑞中美(圖1) ··········· 1小匙

2
魚露 ················· 2大匙
糖 ··················· 1小匙

3
玉米筍、竹筍(罐頭)··· 各¼杯
四季豆(切段) ··········· ¼杯
草菇(罐頭) ············ 10個
九層塔················ 10片
泰國檸檬葉 ·············· 6片

½ 1b. (225g) pork, cut in
pieces

1
1½c. water
1½ T. red curry paste
2 sliced galanga
1 t. rhizome (Fig.1)

2
2 T. fish sauce
1 t. sugar

3
¼ c. ea (canned): bamboo
shoots, baby corn
¼ c. string beans,
cut 1″ (2cm) long
10 canned straw
mushrooms
10 basil leaves
6 kaffir leaves

1 ①料燒開，隨入肉及②、③料再燒開，改中火煮約10分鐘即成。

● 此菜餚不含椰奶；泰式薑及瑞中美是用來加強菜餚之香味。

1 Bring ① to boil. Add meat, ②, and ③ then bring to boil again.
Reduce heat to medium and cook 10 minutes. Serve.

● Coconut milk is not used in this dish. Galanga and rhizome are used
to enhance the flavor.

Fig. 1

Fig. 2

番茄絞肉咖哩
Thai Dip
(Nam Prik Ong)

豬絞肉 ····················· 6兩

① 油、紅咖哩醬 ········ 各1大匙
大乾辣椒(泡軟、剁碎) ··· 1條

② 魚露 ······················ 1大匙
椰子糖 ···················· ½小匙

小番茄(切半) ············· 8粒

½ lb. (225g) ground pork

① 1 T. ea: oil, red curry paste
1 dried New Mexico chili,
softened in cold water
and minced

② 1 T. fish sauce
½ t. palm sugar

8 cherry tomatoes, cut in
half

1 ①料以中火邊攪邊燒煮至有香味,隨入肉炒熟,再依序入②料及番茄燒開,
改中火煮約5分鐘,可與飯或喜好蔬菜配食。

1 Stir-fry ① in medium heat until fragrant. Add pork and stir-fry in
high heat until cooked. Add ② and tomatoes; bring to boil.
Reduce heat to medium and cook 5 minutes. Goes well with one's
favorite vegetables.

青豆牛肉咖哩
Beef Panang

牛肉(切片、見58頁,圖2)6兩

① 油 ······················· 1大匙
潘納咖哩醬 ··········· 1½大匙

② 椰奶···¾杯、魚露 ······ 1大匙
糖 ························· 1小匙

青豆仁·····················½杯

½ lb. (225g) beef, sliced
(Fig.2, P.58)

① 1 T. oil
1½ T. panang curry paste

② ¾ c. coconut milk
1 T. fish sauce
1 t. sugar

½ c. green peas

1 將①料以中火邊攪邊燒煮至有香味,隨入肉、②料及青豆仁大火燒開,改
中火煮約10分鐘即成。

● 可用雞肉或蝦仁取代牛肉。

1 Stir-fry ① in medium heat until fragrant. Add meat, ② and green
peas then bring to boil. Reduce heat to medium and cook 10
minutes. Serve.

● Chicken or shelled shrimp may be substituted for beef.

茄子雞肉咖哩
Chicken & Green Curry with Eggplant

雞肉（切塊）⋯⋯⋯⋯⋯⋯ 6兩

[1]
油 ⋯⋯⋯⋯⋯⋯⋯⋯ 1大匙
綠咖哩醬 ⋯⋯⋯⋯⋯ 1½大匙
椰奶 ⋯⋯⋯⋯⋯⋯⋯ 4大匙

[2]
椰奶 ⋯⋯⋯⋯⋯⋯⋯ 1¼杯
魚露 ⋯⋯⋯⋯⋯⋯⋯ 2大匙
椰子糖 ⋯⋯⋯⋯⋯⋯ 1小匙
泰國檸檬葉 ⋯⋯⋯⋯⋯ 6片

[3]
茄子（圖1）⋯⋯⋯⋯⋯⋯1杯
九層塔 ⋯⋯⋯⋯⋯⋯⋯10片

½ lb. (225g) boneless
  chicken pieces

[1]
1 T. oil
1½ T. green curry paste
4 T. coconut milk

[2]
1¼ c. coconut milk
2 T. fish sauce
1 t. palm sugar
6 kaffir leaves

[3]
1 c. eggplant pieces (Fig.1)
10 basil leaves

1 將[1]料以中火邊攪邊燒煮至有香味，隨入雞肉及[2]料燒開，改中火煮約10分鐘，再加[3]料煮5分鐘即成。

● 若喜歡吃軟一點的茄子，燒煮時間可加長。

1 Stir-fry [1] in medium heat until fragrant. Add chicken and [2] then bring to boil. Reduce heat to medium and cook 10 minutes. Add [3] and cook 5 more minutes. Serve.

● If soft egglpant is preferred, increase cooking time.

Fig.1

Fig.2

Fig.3

洋芋雞腿咖哩
Chicken & Red Curry

1 雞腿(切塊、見60頁，圖2)8兩
1 馬鈴薯(切塊) ············· 1個
洋葱(切塊) ··············· ¼個

2 油…1大匙、椰奶········4大匙
紅咖哩醬 ··········· 1½大匙

3 椰奶…1¼杯、魚露······2大匙
椰子糖 ···············1小匙
咖哩粉、紅椒粉······各¼小匙

1 ⅔ lb. (300g) chicken
  pieces (Fig.2, P.60)
  1 potato, cut in pieces
  ¼ onion, cut in pieces

2 1 T. oil
  1½ T. red curry paste
  4 T. coconut milk

3 1¼ c. coconut milk
  2 T. fish sauce
  1 t. palm sugar
  ¼ t. ea: curry powder,
  paprika powder

1 將2料以中火邊攪邊燒煮至有香味，隨入1、3料大火燒開，改中火煮約25分鐘即成；可與「涼拌黃瓜」(見11頁)配食。

● 如將馬鈴薯改切小塊，燒煮時間可縮短。

1 Stir-fry 2 in medium heat until fragrant. Add 1 and 3 then bring to boil. Reduce heat to medium and cook 25 minutes. May be served with "cucumber sauce" (P.11).

● If potato is cut in small pieces, reduce cooking time.

冬瓜雞肉咖哩
Chicken & Red Curry with Winter Squash

1 雞肉(切塊) ················ 6兩

2 2料同上

3 椰奶…1¼杯、魚露······2大匙
椰子糖、青檸檬汁 ··· 各1小匙
泰國檸檬葉 ··············· 6片

冬瓜(見60頁，圖3)········1杯

1 ½ lb. (225g) boneless
  chicken pieces

2 see 2 in above recipe

3 1¼ c. coconut milk
  2 T. fish sauce
  1 t. palm sugar
  1 t. lime juice
  6 kaffir leaves

  1 c. winter squash
  (Fig.3, P.60)

1 將2料以中火邊攪邊燒煮至有香味，隨入1及3料燒開，改中火煮約10分鐘，再加冬瓜煮10分鐘即成。

● 如無冬瓜可用白蘿蔔取代。

1 Stir-fry 2 in medium heat until fragrant. Add meat and 3 then bring to boil. Reduce heat to medium and cook 10 minutes. Add winter squash and cook 10 more minutes. Serve.

● The shape of winter squash is similar to a large watermelon. Winter squash is sold in pieces at Chinese supermarkets.

咖哩鮭魚
Grilled Salmon Fillet Panang

鮭魚排1片⋯⋯⋯⋯⋯⋯9兩

[1] 油、潘納咖哩醬 ⋯⋯ 各1大匙
椰奶 ⋯⋯⋯⋯⋯⋯⋯ 4大匙

[2] 椰奶⋯⋯⋯⋯⋯⋯⋯½杯
魚露⋯⋯⋯⋯⋯⋯⋯¾大匙
糖⋯⋯⋯⋯⋯⋯⋯⋯1小匙
紅椒粉⋯⋯⋯⋯⋯⋯½小匙

[3] 椰奶漿 ⋯⋯⋯⋯⋯⋯1大匙
泰國檸檬葉(切絲) ⋯⋯⋯ 4片

1 salmon fillet, ¾ 1b.
(340g)

[1] 1 T. oil
1 T. panang curry paste
4 T. coconut milk

[2] ½ c. coconut milk
¾ T. fish sauce
1 t. sugar
½ t. paprika powder

[3] 1 T. thick coconut milk
4 kaffir leaves, shredded

1 鮭魚在炭火上(或用烤箱)烤熟。

2 將[1]料以中火邊攪邊燒煮至有香味,隨入[2]料大火燒開,澆在烤好的魚排上,淋上[3]料即成。

1 Grill or bake salmon until cooked.

2 Stir-fry [1] in medium heat until fragrant. Add [2] and bring sauce to boil. Pour the sauce then [3] over fillet and serve.

鳳梨蝦咖哩
Shrimp & Pineapple Curry

蝦（無殼） ···················· 6兩

1 |
油 ·························· 1大匙
紅咖哩醬 ·············· 1½大匙
椰奶 ······················ 4大匙

2 |
椰奶 ······················ 1¼杯
魚露 ······················ 2大匙
糖、醋 ·················· 各1小匙
紅椒粉 ·····················¼小匙
泰國檸檬葉（圖1）··········4片

新鮮或罐頭鳳梨（切碎）··· 1杯

½ 1b. (225g) shelled shrimp

1 |
1 T. oil
1½ T. red curry paste
4 T. coconut milk

2 |
1¼ c. coconut milk
2 T. fish sauce
1 t. ea: sugar, vinegar
¼ t. paprika powder
4 kaffir leaves (Fig.1)

1 c. fresh or canned
pineapple, minced

1 蝦抽去腸泥，洗淨後瀝乾水份。

2 將1料以中火邊攪邊燒煮至有香味，依序入2料及鳳梨大火燒開後，再加蝦煮熟即成。

● 獻給對鳳梨口味特別喜愛的人。

1 Devein shrimp; rinse and drain.

2 Stir-fry 1 in medium heat until fragrant. Add 2 and pineapple then bring to boil. Add shrimp and cook until color changes; serve.

● This dish is popular with people who enjoy pineapple flavor.

Fig.1

筍片牛肉咖哩
Beef & Green Curry

牛肉(切片) ················· 6兩

1
油 ······················ 1大匙
綠咖哩醬 ················ 1½大匙
椰奶 ····················· 4大匙

2
椰奶 ····················· 1¼杯
魚露 ····················· 2大匙
椰子糖 ··················· 1小匙

3
筍片(罐頭) ·············· 1杯
青豆仁 ··················· ¼杯
泰國檸檬葉 ··············· 6片
九層塔 ··················· 10片

½ lb. (225g) beef, cut in pieces

1
1 T. oil
1½ T. green curry paste
4 T. coconut milk

2
1¼ c. coconut milk
2 T. fish sauce
1 t. palm sugar

3
1 c. canned bamboo shoots
¼ c. green peas
6 kaffir leaves
10 basil leaves

1 將1料以中火邊攪邊燒煮至有香味，隨入肉及2、3料大火燒開，改中火煮約10分鐘即成。

● 3料見圖1。泰國檸檬葉及九層塔是加強菜餚的香味。

1 Stir-fry 1 in medium heat until fragrant. Add meat, 2, and 3 then bring to boil. Reduce heat to medium and cook 10 minutes. Serve.

● See Fig. 1 for 3. Kaffir and basil leaves enhance the flavor of the dish.

Fig. 1

南瓜牛肉咖哩
Beef & Red Curry with Pumpkin

牛肉（切片）⋯⋯⋯⋯⋯⋯ 6兩

1　油 ⋯⋯⋯⋯⋯⋯⋯⋯⋯⋯ 1大匙
　　紅咖哩醬 ⋯⋯⋯⋯⋯⋯ 1½大匙
　　椰奶 ⋯⋯⋯⋯⋯⋯⋯⋯ 4大匙

2　椰奶 ⋯⋯⋯⋯⋯⋯⋯⋯⋯ 1¼杯
　　魚露 ⋯⋯⋯⋯⋯⋯⋯⋯⋯ 2大匙
　　椰子糖 ⋯⋯⋯⋯⋯⋯⋯⋯ 1小匙
　　紅椒粉 ⋯⋯⋯⋯⋯⋯⋯⋯ ¼小匙
　　泰國檸檬葉 ⋯⋯⋯⋯⋯⋯ 6片

南瓜（圖1）⋯⋯⋯⋯⋯⋯⋯ 1杯

½ 1b. (225g) beef, cut in
　pieces

1　1 T. oil
　　1½ T. red curry paste
　　4 T. coconut milk

2　1¼ c. coconut milk
　　2 T. fish sauce
　　1 t. palm sugar
　　¼ t. paprika powder
　　6 kaffir leaves

1 c. pumpkin (Fig.1)

1 1 料以中火邊攪邊燒煮至有香味，隨入牛肉及 2 料燒開，改中火煮約10分鐘，再加南瓜煮5分鐘即成。

● 南瓜切時很硬，但很容易煮爛，煮軟後可連皮食用。

1 Stir-fry 1 in medium heat until fragrant. Add beef and 2 then bring to boil. Reduce heat to medium and cook 10 minutes. Add pumpkin and cook 5 more minutes. Serve.

● Pumpkin is hard to cut but easily softened by cooking. When softened, may be eaten with its skin.

Fig. 1

65

花生牛肉咖哩
Masaman Beef

1	牛肉(切塊、圖1)‥‥‥‥‥6兩 花生(圖1)‥‥‥‥‥‥3大匙 水‥‥‥‥‥‥‥‥‥‥7杯

馬鈴薯(切塊)‥‥‥‥‥1個

2	油‥‥‥‥‥‥‥‥‥‥1大匙 瑪沙門咖哩醬(圖2)‥1½大匙 椰奶‥‥‥‥‥‥‥‥‥4大匙

3	椰奶‥‥‥‥‥‥‥‥1¼杯 魚露‥‥‥‥‥‥‥‥‥2大匙 椰子糖、青檸檬汁‥各1小匙 紅椒粉‥‥‥‥‥‥‥‥¼小匙

洋葱(切塊)‥‥‥‥‥‥¼個

1 ½ lb. (225g) beef, cut in
  pieces (Fig.1)
  3 T. peanuts (Fig.1)
  7 c. water

  1 potato, cut in pieces

2 1 T. oil
  1½ T. masaman curry
  paste (Fig.2)
  4 T. coconut milk

3 1¼ c. coconut milk
  2 T. fish sauce
  1 t. ea: palm sugar, lime juice
  ¼ t. paprika powder

  ¼ onion, cut in pieces

1 1 料燒開，改小火煮40分鐘後，放入馬鈴薯續煮20分鐘，即熄火。

2 將 2 料以中火邊攪邊煮至有香味，加入上列煮好的全部材料及 3 料大火燒開，改小火煮約10分鐘後，再加洋葱略煮即成。可與「涼拌黃瓜(見11頁)配食。

1 Bring 1 to boil. Reduce heat to low and cook 40 minutes. Add potato and cook another 20 minutes.

2 Stir-fry 2 in medium heat until fragrant. Add 1 and 3 then bring to boil. Reduce heat to low and cook 10 minutes. Add onion and cook briefly. May be served with "cucumber salad" (P.10).

Fig 1

Fig 2

Fig 3

Fig 4

鑲黃瓜湯
Stuffed
Cucumber Soup

黃瓜（削皮）⋯⋯⋯⋯⋯⋯ 1 條

1 豬絞肉 ⋯⋯⋯⋯⋯⋯⋯⋯ 3 兩
白醬油¾大匙、太白粉¼小匙

高湯（或水）⋯⋯⋯⋯⋯⋯ 2½杯

2 魚露 ⋯⋯⋯⋯⋯⋯⋯⋯⋯ 1 大匙
白醬油⋯⋯⋯⋯⋯⋯⋯⋯ ¼大匙

3 葱花⋯⋯⋯⋯⋯⋯⋯⋯⋯ ½大匙
胡椒⋯⋯⋯⋯⋯⋯⋯⋯⋯ 適量

1 peeled cucumber

1 ¼ **lb. (115g) ground pork**
¾ **T. thin soy sauce**
¼ **t. cornstarch**

2½ **c. stock or water**

2 1 **T. fish sauce**
¼ **T. thin soy sauce**

3 ½ **T. chopped green onion**
pepper as desired

1 黃瓜切6等份、去籽（見66頁，圖3）。1料調勻成肉餡。

2 黃瓜在內緣抹上少許太白粉，用肉餡填滿。

3 鑲黃瓜加高湯燒開後，改中火蓋鍋煮30分鐘至湯剩約2杯，加入2料略攪，撒上3料即成。

1 Cut cucumber into 6 pieces. Remove seeds (Fig.3, P.66). Mix 1 to make filling.

2 Lightly sprinkle cornstarch into cavities of cucumber then stuff them with filling.

3 Add stock to filled cucmber then bring to boil. Cover and cook over medium heat 30 minutes until soup is reduced to 2 cups. Add 2 and sprinkle with 3; serve.

豆腐湯
Tofu Soup

1 豬絞肉 ⋯⋯⋯⋯⋯⋯⋯⋯ 3 兩
大白菜、豆腐 ⋯⋯⋯ 切塊各3兩
乾粉絲（泡軟）⋯⋯⋯⋯⋯⅔兩
草菇（罐頭）⋯⋯⋯⋯⋯⋯ 10個

高湯（或水）⋯⋯⋯⋯⋯⋯ 2 杯

2、3料同上

4 糖、蒜油⋯⋯⋯⋯⋯⋯ 各½小匙
芫荽⋯⋯⋯⋯⋯⋯⋯⋯⋯ 適量

1 ¼ **lb. (115g) ground pork**
¼ **lb. (115g) ea (cut in pieces): nappa cabbage, bean curd (tofu)**
1 **oz. (28g) dried bean threads, softened in cold water**
10 canned straw mushrooms

2 **c. stock or water**

2,3 see 2,3 in above recipe

4 ½ **t. ea: sugar, garlic oil cilantro as desired**

1 將高湯燒開，依序入1、2料煮至肉熟，再加3、4料即成。

● 是一道清湯，對老人、幼兒均適合。

● 1料見66頁，圖4。

1 Bring stock to boil. Add 1 and 2; cook until meat changes color. Add 3 and 4; serve.

● This light soup is a favorite with young and old alike.

● See Fig.4, P.66 for 1.

酸辣白菜湯
Spicy Nappa Cabbage Soup (Kang Som)

1
魚肉（切塊）	6兩
大白菜（切塊）	2杯

2
卡森咖哩醬	1小匙
大乾辣椒	半條
乾辣椒	1條
蝦醬	½小匙
洋葱絲	1大匙
蒜	2瓣
塩	⅛小匙
水	⅔杯

3
水	½杯
魚露	1大匙
青檸檬汁、酸子汁	各1大匙
糖	½小匙

1
- ½ 1b. (225g) fish fillet, cut in pieces
- 2 c. nappa cabbage, cut in pieces

2
- 1 t. kang som curry paste
- ½ dried New Mexican chili
- 1 dried chili
- ½ t. shrimp paste
- 1 T. shredded onion
- 2 garlic cloves
- ⅛ t. salt
- ⅔ c. water

3
- ½ c. water
- 1 T. ea: fish sauce, lime juice, tamarind juice
- ½ t. sugar

1 將②料在果汁機內攪爛後，加③料燒開，再加①料煮至魚肉熟即成。

● ②料見圖1。①料可隨意變換，如蝦可取代魚，蔬菜可用花菜，白蘿蔔、玉米筍、包心菜、毛菇等來取代。

1 Liquify ② in a blender. Add ③ and bring to boil. Add ①; cook until fish changes color. Serve.

● See Fig. 1 for ②. Shrimp may be substituted for fish. Cauliflower, white radish, baby corn, cabbage, mushrooms, etc. may be substituted for nappa cabbage.

Fig. 1

酸辣蝦湯

Spicy Shrimp Soup (Tom Yum Koong)

① 蝦（無殼）······ 4兩
　毛菇（切半）······ 8個
　草菇（罐頭）······12個

② 高湯 ······ 2杯
　香茅（切段）······½根
　泰國檸檬葉、泰式薑 ··· 各4片
　辣椒 ······ 4-6條

③ 魚露、青檸檬汁 ······ 各2大匙
　糖、辣椒膏··········各½小匙

　芫荽··················適量

① ⅓ 1b. (150g) shelled shrimp
　　with tail
　8 mushrooms, cut in half
　12 canned straw mushrooms

② 2 c. stock
　½ lemon grass,
　　cut 1″ (2cm) long
　4 slices ea: kaffir leaves,
　　galanga
　4-6 chilies

③ 2 T. fish sauce
　2 T lime juice
　½ t. ea: sugar, chili paste
　　with soya bean oil

cilantro as desired

1 蝦抽去腸泥，洗淨後瀝乾水份。

2 將②料燒開後依序入①、③料，煮至蝦熟撒上芫荽即成。

● 食後會帶給您滿足感的泰國酸辣湯。

● ②料見圖1，香茅處理法見71頁。

1 Devein shrimp; rinse and drain.

2 Bring ② to boil; add ① and ③; cook until shrimp changes color.
　Sprinkle with cilantro; serve.

● This spicy Thai soup will satisfy your palate.

● See Fig. 1 for ②. See P.71 for preparing lemon grass.

Fig. 1

蔬菜蝦湯
Shrimp & Zucchini Soup

|1| 蝦（無殼） ···················· 4兩
菠菜 ······················· 8片
義大利瓜（切塊）··········½條
玉米筍、草菇（罐頭）···共½杯

|2| 洋蔥絲、水 ··············各¼杯
胡椒、蝦醬 ··········各½小匙
蝦米 ····················· 1大匙

|3| 水 ·······················1½杯
魚露 ······················ 1大匙
糖··························½小匙

九層塔······················10片

|1| ⅓ 1b. (150g) shelled shrimp with tail
8 leaves of spinach
½ zucchini, cut in pieces
total of ½ c.: canned baby corn, canned straw mushrooms

|2| ¼ c. shredded onion
¼ c. water
½ t. pepper
½ t. shrimp paste
1 T. dried shrimp

|3| 1½ c. water
1 T. fish sauce
½ t. sugar

10 basil leaves

1 蝦抽去腸泥，洗淨後瀝乾水份。

2 將|2|料在果汁機內攪爛後加|3|料燒開，去除泡沫，入|1|料煮至蝦熟，撒上九層塔即成。

● |1|料見圖1。

1 Devein shrimp; rinse and drain.

2 Stir |2| in a blender. Add |3| and bring to boil. Remove residue from surface. Add |1| and cook until shrimp changes color. Sprinkle with basil leaves; serve.

● See Fig. 1 for |1|

Fig. 1

雞肉椰奶湯
Chicken Coconut Soup (Tom Kah Kai)

│1)⋯⋯⋯⋯4兩
│圖1)⋯⋯ 20個
⋯⋯⋯⋯⋯ 1½杯
⋯⋯⋯⋯⋯ ½杯

2 香茅⋯⋯⋯⋯⋯⋯ ½根
泰國檸檬葉、泰式薑(圖2)各4片
辣椒 ⋯⋯⋯⋯⋯⋯ 6條

3 魚露、青檸檬汁 ⋯⋯ 各2大匙

4 蔥花 ⋯⋯⋯⋯⋯⋯ 1大匙
苑荽⋯⋯⋯⋯⋯⋯⋯ 適量

1 ⅓ 1b. (150g) boneless
chicken, cut in strips (Fig.1)
20 canned straw
mushrooms (Fig.1)

2 1½ c. coconut milk
½ c. water
½ lemon grass,
cut 1″ (2cm) long
4 ea: kaffir leaves, sliced
galanga (Fig.2)
6 chilies

3 2 T. fish sauce
2 T. lime juice

4 1 T. chopped green onion
cilantro as desired

Fig. 1

Fig. 2

Fig. 3

1 將2料燒開，依序入1、3料，煮至肉熟，撒上4料即成。這是最有泰國獨特風味的湯。

● 香茅的處理法：需先去除老皮，上端較嫩的部份切碎，用在沙拉內；下端較老的部份，切段用在湯內(圖3)。

1 Bring 2 to boil. Add 1 and 3; cook until meat changes color. Sprinkle with 4; serve. This is one of Thailand's most uniquely flavored and popular soups.

● Preparing lemon grass: Trim off the hard skin. Mince upper tenderer portion for salad. Cut the lower harder portion in pieces for soup (Fig.3).

辣味冬粉湯
Spicy Silver Noodle Soup

1
- 豬絞肉 ⋯⋯⋯⋯⋯⋯⋯ 2兩
- 蝦仁、魚餅(切片) ⋯⋯ 共4兩
- 魚丸 ⋯⋯⋯⋯⋯⋯⋯⋯ 4個
- 乾粉絲(泡軟) ⋯⋯⋯⋯⋯ ⅔兩

2
- 魚露 ⋯⋯⋯⋯⋯⋯⋯ 1½大匙
- 冬菜、醋 ⋯⋯⋯⋯⋯ 各1小匙
- 糖、蒜油 ⋯⋯⋯⋯⋯ 各½小匙
- 辣椒粉 ⋯⋯⋯⋯⋯⋯⋯ ¼小匙

3
- 豆芽菜 ⋯⋯⋯⋯⋯⋯⋯ 1杯
- 葱花 ⋯⋯⋯⋯⋯⋯⋯ 1大匙

4
- 碎花生 ⋯⋯⋯⋯⋯⋯⋯ 1大匙
- 芫荽、辣椒粒、胡椒 ⋯⋯ 適量

1
- 3 oz. (84g) ground pork
- total of ⅓ lb. (150g):
    shelled shrimp, sliced
    fried fish cake
- 4 fish balls
- 1 oz (28g) bean threads,
    softened in cold water

2
- 1½ T. fish sauce
- 1 t. preserved cabbage
- 1 t. vinegar
- ½ t. ea: sugar, garlic oil
- ¼ t. ground chili

3
- 1 c. bean sprouts
- 1 T. chopped green onion

4
- 1 T. crushed peanuts
- cilantro, pepper, and
    chopped chili as desired

1 蝦抽去腸泥，洗淨後瀝乾水份。

2 水2杯燒開，隨入肉煮熟，去除白沫，隨入 1 料燒開後，依序入 2 、 3 料再燒開，撒上 4 料即成。

● 1 料見圖1。

1 Devein shrimp; rinse and drain.

2 Bring 2 cups of water to boil; add meat and cook until color changes. Remove scum. Add 1 and bring to boil. Add 2 and 3 then bring to another boil. Sprinkle with 4 ; serve.

● See Fig. 1 for 1

Fig. 1

Fig. 2

Fig. 3

什錦拌麵
Egg Noodles with Pork & Fish Balls

蛋麵 ····························· 3兩

|1| 冬菜、蠔油 ·········· 各1小匙
    蒜油 ····················· 2小匙

|2| 魚露 ····························· ¾大匙
    糖、醋 ················· 各1小匙

烤豬肉(切片) ············· 2兩

|3| 青梗菜 ······1棵、魚丸 ······6個
    炸魚餅(切片) ············· 2兩

|4| 葱、辣椒、芫荽、胡椒 ··· 適量

¼ lb. (115g) egg noodles

|1| 1 t. ea: preserved cabbage, oyster sauce
    2 t. garlic oil

|2| ¾ T. fish sauce
    1 t. ea: sugar, vinegar

3 oz. (84g) roast pork, sliced

|3| 1 bok choy, 6 fish balls
    3 oz. (84g) fried fish cake, sliced

|4| chopped green onions, chili, cilantro and pepper as desired

1 蛋麵入滾水內燒開即撈出，與|1|、|2|料拌勻分盛入麵碗內。

2 將|3|料分別在滾水內燙熟，與烤豬肉擺在麵上，上撒|4|料即成。

● 蛋麵見72頁，圖2，若使用其他種麵，則按包裝上指示將麵煮熟；青梗菜見72頁，圖3。

1 Put noodles in boiling water, bring to boil again. Remove and drain noodles then mix with |1| and |2|. Distribute noodles into bowls.

2 Cook |3| separately in boiling water; remove and place with roast pork over noodles. Sprinkle with |4|; serve.

● See Fig.2, P.72 for egg noodles. If different noodles are used, follow instructions on package. See Fig.3, P.72 for bok choy.

什錦湯麵
Egg Noodles with Pork & Fish Ballsp

蛋麵(見72頁，圖2) ········3兩

|2| 高湯 ···4杯、魚露 ······1¾大匙
    糖、醋 ················· 各1小匙

蝦(無殼) ····················· 2兩

|1|、|3|、|4|料同上

¼ lb. (115g) egg noodles (Fig.2, P.72)

|2| 4 c. stock
    1¾ T. fish sauce
    1 t. ea: sugar, vinegar

3 oz. (84g) shelled shrimp with tail

|1|,|3|,|4|, see |1|,|3|,|4|, in above recipe

1 蝦抽去腸泥，洗淨後瀝乾水份；蛋麵放入滾水內燒開即撈出，與|1|料拌勻分盛入麵碗內。

2 將蝦及|3|料分別在滾水內煮熟，撈出擺在麵上。

3 將|2|料燒開，澆在麵上，上撒|4|料即成。

1 Devein shrimp; rinse and drain. Put noodles in boiling water, bring to boil again. Remove and drain noodles then mix with |1|. Distribute noodles into bowls.

2 Cook shrimp and |3| separately in boiling water; remove and place over noodles.

3 Bring |2| to boil; pour over noodles. Sprinkle with |1|; serve.

燴河粉 I

Pork Slices over Rice Noodles (Rad Na)

豬肉(切片) ················· 6兩

1 | 白醬油、酒、太白粉 各1小匙

麻油(圖1) ···············1大匙
河粉(圖2) ············· 12兩

2 | 蒜末、豆瓣醬 ········ 各1小匙

芥蘭菜(切段) ············· 3兩

3 | 蠔油、白醬油········各¾大匙
甜醬油、糖、醋 ······ 各1小匙

4 | 高湯(或水) ···········10大匙
太白粉 ················· 2小匙

½ 1b. (225g) sliced pork

1 | 1 t. ea: thin soy sauce,
cooking wine, cornstarch

1 T. sesame oil (Fig.1)
1 1b. (450g) rice noodle
sheets (Fig.2)

2 | 1 t. ea: minced garlic, soy
bean condiment

¼ 1b. (115g) Chinese
broccoli, cut 2″ (5cm) long

3 | ¾ T. ea: oyster sauce, thin
soy sauce
1 t. ea: sweet soy sauce,
sugar, vinegar

4 | 10 T. stock or water
2 t. cornstarch

1 肉拌入 1 料略醃。河粉切條後用手一片片分開。

2 麻油燒熱,將河粉炒熱,分盛入盤。

3 油2大匙燒熱,炒香 2 料,隨入肉炒熟,依序入芥蘭菜及 3 料拌炒後,再加調勻的 4 料勾汁,澆在河粉上即成。

1 Marinate pork with 1 . Cut rice sheets in strips then separate.

2 Heat sesame oil then stir-fry strips until hot. Place on plates.

3 Heat 2 T. oil then stir-fry 2 until fragrant. Add meat; stir until color changes. Add Chinese broccoli and 3 then stir-fry briefly; thicken with mixed 4 . Pour over rice noodle strips; serve.

Fig. 1

Fig. 2

燴河粉 II
Ground Beef over Rice Noodles

牛絞肉 ································· 6兩
河粉（見74頁、圖2）······ 12兩

1 咖哩粉 ···························· ½小匙
冬菜、蒜末 ············ 各1小匙

2 洋蔥、青椒、紅蘿蔔、芹菜、
番茄 ··············· 切片共2杯

3 白醬油 ····················· 1½大匙
甜醬油、糖、醋 ······ 各1小匙

4 高湯（或水）············10大匙
太白粉 ····················· 2小匙

½ lb. (225g) ground beef
1 lb. (450g) rice noodle
　sheets (P.74, Fig.2)

1 ½ t. curry powder
1 t. ea: preserved cabbage,
　minced garlic

2 total of 2 c. (sliced): onion,
　green bell pepper,
　carrot, celery, tomato

3 1½ T. thin soy sauce
1 t. ea: sweet soy sauce,
　sugar, vinegar

4 10 T. stock or water
2 t. cornstarch

1 河粉切條後用手一片片分開。

2 油1大匙燒熱，將河粉炒熱，分盛入盤。

3 油2大匙燒熱，炒香 1 料，隨入肉略炒、依序入 2 、 3 料拌炒後，再加調勻的 4 料勾汁，澆在河粉上，可與「辣椒醬」（見8頁）配食。

1 Cut rice noodle sheets in strips then separate.

2 Heat 1 T. oil then stir-fry strips until hot. Distribute onto plates.

3 Heat 2 T. oil then stir-fry 1 until fragrant; add meat and stir-fry briefly. Add 2 and 3 ; stir to mix well. Thicken with mixed 4 . Pour over noodle strips. May be served with "chili paste" (P.8).

炒河粉 I

Fried Rice Noodles & Beef (Pad See Eaw)

牛肉(切片) ················· 6兩
1 白醬油、酒、太白粉 各1小匙
河粉(見74頁，圖2) ······ 12兩
2 蒜末、豆瓣醬 ········· 各1小匙
青花菜(切塊) ·············· 1杯
　白醬油 ················· 1½大匙
3 甜醬油 ··················· 2小匙
　糖、醋 ················· 各1小匙
豆芽 ····················· 4兩

½ lb. (225g) sliced beef

1 | 1 t. ea: thin soy sauce,
cooking wine, cornstarch

1 lb. (450g) rice noodle
sheets (P.74, Fig.2)

2 | 1 t. ea: minced garlic, soy
bean condiment

1 c. broccoli, cut in pieces

3 | 1½ T. thin soy sauce
2 t. sweet soy sauce
1 t. ea: sugar, vinegar

⅓ lb. (150g) bean sprouts

1 肉拌入 1 料略醃。河粉切條後用手一片片分開。

2 油1大匙燒熱，將河粉炒熱即取出。

3 油2大匙燒熱，炒香 2 料，隨入肉略炒，依序入青花菜及 3 料炒拌後，再加豆芽及河粉翻拌即成，可與「辣椒醋」(見11頁)配食。

1 Marinate meat with 1 . Cut rice sheets in strips then separate.

2 Heat 1 T. oil then stir-fry strips until hot; remove.

3 Heat 2 T. oil then stir-fry 2 until fragrant. Add meat and stir-fry briefly. Add broccoli and 3 then stir to mix; add bean sprouts and noodle strips, then stir-fry briefly. May be served with "chili vinegar sauce" (P.11).

炒河粉 II
Fried Rice Noodles & Chicken

雞肉(切條) ················· 6兩
河粉(見74頁、圖2) ······ 12兩
1 | 冬菜、蒜末 ············ 各1小匙
蛋 ·························· 2個
2 | 魚露 ··················· 1½大匙
白醬油、糖、醋 ······ 各1小匙
3 | 葱絲 ·····················¼杯
豆芽 ·····················4兩
碎花生 ·················· 1大匙

½ lb. (225g) boneless
   chicken, cut in strips
1 lb. (450g) rice noodle
   sheets (P.74, Fig.2)

1 | 1 t. ea: preserved cabbage,
      minced garlic

2 eggs

2 | 1½ T. fish sauce
    1 t. ea: thin soy sauce,
       sugar, vinegar

3 | ¼ c. green onions,
       cut 1″ (2cm) long
    ⅓ lb. (150g) bean sprouts
    1 T. crushed peanuts

1 河粉切條後，用手一片片分開。油1大匙燒熱，將河粉炒熱。

2 油2大匙燒熱，炒香1料，隨入肉炒熟，續入蛋炒至略乾，依序入2、3料
及河粉拌炒均勻即成，可與「辣椒醋」(見11頁)配食。

1 Cut rice noodle sheets in strips then separate. Heat 1 T. oil then
stir-fry strips until hot; remove.

2 Heat 2 T. oil then stir-fry 1 until fragrant; add meat and stir-fry
until color changes. Add eggs and stir-fry until slightly dry. Add
2, 3, and noodle strips; stir to mix. May be served with "chili
vinegar sauce" (P.11).

炒麵
Fried Thai Noodles (Pad Thai)

豬肉(切片) ················· 3兩
蝦(無殼) ················· 3兩
濕泰國麵 ·················· 12兩
1 | 辣椒、蒜末 ········· 各1小匙
　 | 蛋 ····················· 2個
2 | 魚露、酸子汁 ······ 各1½大匙
　 | 糖 ···················· 1大匙
　 | 紅椒粉 ················· ¼小匙
3 | 薑絲 ···················· ¼杯
　 | 豆芽 ··················· 4兩
　 | 碎花生 ················· 1大匙

¼ lb. (115g) sliced pork
¼ lb. (115g) shelled shrimp
1 lb. (450g) wet sen lek
    noodles

1 | 1 t. ea (minced): garlic, chili

    2 eggs

2 | 1½ T. ea: fish sauce,
    | tamarind juice
    | 1 T. sugar
    | ¼ t. paprika powder

3 | ¼ c. shredded ginger
    | ⅓ lb. (150g) bean sprouts
    | 1 T. crushed peanuts

1 蝦抽去腸泥，洗淨後瀝乾水份。油1大匙燒熱，將麵炒熱。

2 油2大匙燒熱，炒香 1 料，隨入肉、蝦炒熟，續入蛋炒至略乾，依序入 2 、 3 料及麵拌炒均勻即成，可淋上靑檸檬汁。

● 乾泰國麵(圖1)6兩用水泡軟後，增加爲2倍約12兩，如無可用米粉取代，炒時太乾可加3大匙水。

1 Devein shrimp; rinse and drain. Heat 1 T. oil then stir-fry noodles until hot.

2 Heat 2 T. oil then stir-fry 1 until fragrant; add meat and shrimp then stir-fry until color changes. Add eggs and stir-fry until slightly dry. Add 2 , 3 , and noodles then stir-fry briefly. May sprinkle on lime juice; serve.

● ½ lb. (225g) dry Sen Lek Noodles (Fig. 1) soaked and softened in cold water will double in weight to 1 lb. (450g). These noodles may be substituted with thin rice noodles; add 3 T. water if too dry during stir-frying.

Fig. 1

泰式意大利麵
Thai Spaghetti

雞絞肉 ······················ 6兩
乾意大利麵 ················ 4兩

1. 冬菜、蒜末 ··········· 各1小匙
   辣椒（切絲）················ 6條

2. 洋葱、青椒、番茄 ······ 共2杯
   九層塔·······················20片

3. 魚露 ····················· 1½大匙
   甜醬油、糖、醋 ······ 各1小匙

4. 高湯（或水）·············10大匙
   太白粉 ····················· 2小匙

½ lb. (225g) ground chicken
⅓ lb. (150g) spaghetti (Fig.1)

1. 1 t. ea: preserved cabbage,
      minced garlic
   6 shredded chilies

2. total of 2 c.: onion, green
      bell pepper, tomato
   20 basil leaves

3. 1½ T. fish sauce
   1 t. ea: sweet soy sauce,
      sugar, vinegar

4. 10 T. stock or water
   2 t. cornstarch

1 水燒開，放入意大利麵煮熟，撈出瀝乾，與油1大匙翻拌，分盛入盤內。

2 油2大匙燒熱，炒香①料，隨入肉炒熟，依序入②、③料拌炒後再加調勻的④料勾汁，澆在麵上即成。

● 乾意大利麵（圖1），可按包裝上指示將麵煮熟。

1 Follow package instructions and cook spaghetti. Remove and drain, then mix with 1 T. oil. Distribute noodles into bowls.

2 Heat 2 T. oil then stir-fry ① until fragrant. Add meat and stir-fry until color changes. Add ② and ③ then stir to mix; thicken with mixed ④ then pour over spaghetti.

Fig. 1

蝦粥
Shrimp & Porridge

蝦（無殼） ·················· 4兩
蛋（打散） ·················· 1個

1 | 飯 ························· 1杯
　　| 高湯 ······················· 2杯
　　| 薑絲 ······················ 1大匙

2 | 魚露 ······················ 1大匙
　　| 糖、醋 ··················· 各½小匙
　　| 冬菜（圖1） ················· 1小匙

3 | 葱花、芹菜丁 ········ 各1大匙
　　| 芫荽 ······················· 適量

⅓ lb. (150g) shelled shrimp
　with tails
1 beaten egg

1 | 1 c. cooked rice
　　| 2 c. stock
　　| 1 T. shredded ginger

2 | 1 T. fish sauce
　　| ½ t. ea: sugar, vinegar
　　| 1 t. preserved cabbage
　　　(Fig.1)

3 | 1 T. ea (chopped): green
　　　onion, celery
　cilantro as desired

1 蝦抽去腸泥，洗淨後瀝乾水份。蛋液煎成蛋皮後切絲。

2 將 1 料燒開，依序入蝦、2 料煮至蝦熟，撒上蛋絲及 3 料即成。

● 如有現成的白飯，可加高湯及調味料煮成粥，是一道不費時的速簡午餐。

1 Devein shrimp; rinse and drain, Fry egg to form a pancake then shred.

2 Bring 1 to boil; add shrimp then 2 ; cook until shrimp changes color. Sprinkle with egg shreds and 3 ; serve.

● To make porridge, bring stock and cooked rice to boil. Shrimp, egg, meat, or vegetables may be added if desired.

Fig. 1

絞肉粥
Ground Pork & Porridge

1 豬絞肉 ····················· 4兩
白醬油 ····················· ½大匙

蛋 ·························· 1個

2 飯 ·························· 1杯
高湯(或水) ················ 2杯
薑絲 ······················· 1大匙

3 魚露 ······················ 1大匙
糖、醋 ··················· 各½小匙
蒜油(見9頁) ·············· 1小匙

4 葱花 ······················ 1大匙
芫荽、胡椒 ················· 適量

1 ⅓ lb. (150g) ground pork
½ T. thin soy sauce

1 egg

2 1 c. cooked rice
2 c. stock or water
1 T. shredded ginger

3 1 T. fish sauce
½ t. ea: sugar, vinegar
1 t. garlic oil (P.9)

4 1 T. chopped green onions
cilantro and pepper as
desired

1 1料拌勻,蛋放入湯碗內。

2 2料在果汁機內攪爛,與3料放入鍋內煮開,再入拌勻1料略攪至熟,撒上4料倒入蛋碗內即成。

● 如在粥內加少許炸過的蝦米味更香。

1 Mix 1 well. Put egg in a soup bowl.

2 Stir 2 in blender. Mix 2 and 3, bring to boil. Add 1 and stir briefly until cooked. Sprinkle with 4; pour over the egg. Serve.

● Dry shrimp, deep-fried, may be added to porridge for extra flavor.

雞汁飯
Chicken & Garlic Rice

雞胸1個（帶骨、皮切半） 12兩

|1| 鹽 ……………………… 1小匙
水 ……………………… 4杯
芫荽莖（切碎） ………… 1大匙

|2| 蒜（略拍） ……………… 2瓣
長米（不洗） …………… 1½杯

|3| 醬油 …………………… 4大匙
糖、醋、薑末 ………… 各1小匙
豆瓣醬、辣椒末 ……… 各1大匙

1 lb. (450g) chicken breast, cut in half

|1| 1 t. salt
4 c. water
1 T. minced cilantro root

|2| 2 garlic cloves, slightly crushed
1½ c. unwashed long rice

|3| 4 T. soy sauce
1 t. ea: sugar, vinegar, minced ginger
1 T. ea: soy bean condiment , minced chili

1 |1|料燒開後，放入雞胸中火煮15分鐘至肉熟，取出後去骨切片，雞湯留用。

2 油2大匙燒熱，隨入|2|料（圖1）中火將米炒15分鐘取出與雞湯2½杯入電鍋內煮熟。

3 飯與雞片置盤，沾|3|料食用，可與喜好蔬菜配食。

1 Bring |1| to boil; add chicken breast and cook in medium heat 15 minutes; remove chicken and reserve liquid. Remove and discard chicken bones then slice the meat.

2 Heat 2 T. oil then add |2| (Fig. 1). Stir-fry rice over medium heat for 15 minutes; remove and then cook with 2½ c. reserved liquid in a rice cooker.

3 Place rice and chicken slices on a plate; serve with |3| dipping sauce. May also be served with favorite vegetables.

Fig. 1

蘆筍燴飯
Chicken & Asparagus over Rice

雞肉(切條) ⋯⋯⋯⋯⋯⋯ 6兩

1 | 白醬油、酒、太白粉 各1小匙

香腸(切片) ⋯⋯⋯⋯⋯⋯ ½條
蒜末⋯⋯⋯⋯⋯⋯⋯⋯⋯ ½小匙

2 | 蘆筍(切段)
紅蘿蔔、毛菇(切片) ⋯ 共2杯

3 | 魚露、蠔油⋯⋯⋯⋯⋯ 各¾大匙
甜醬油、糖、醋 ⋯⋯⋯ 各1小匙

4 | 高湯(或水)⋯⋯⋯⋯⋯ 10大匙
太白粉 ⋯⋯⋯⋯⋯⋯⋯ 2小匙

飯 ⋯⋯⋯⋯⋯⋯⋯⋯⋯ 2杯

½ lb. (225g) boneless
chicken, cut in strips

1 | 1 t. ea: thin soy sause,
cooking wine, cornstarch

½ Chinese sausage, sliced
½ t. minced garlic

2 | total of 2 c.: asparagus
sections, carrot, &
mushroom slices

3 | ¾ T. fish sauce
¾ T. oyster sauce
1 t. ea: sweet soy sauce,
sugar, vinegar

4 | 10 T. stock or water
2 t. cornstarch

2 c. cooked rice

1 雞肉拌入 1 料略醃。

2 油2大匙燒熱,炒香蒜,隨入肉與香腸炒熟,依序入 2 、 3 料炒拌後,再加調勻的 4 料勾芡,澆在熱飯上,可與「辣椒醋」(見11頁)配食。

● 2 料見圖1。

1 Marinate chicken with 1 .

2 Heat 2 T. oil then stir-fry garlic until fragrant. Add meat and sausage; stir-fry until cooked. Add 2 then 3 ; stir to mix. Thicken with mixture 4 then pour on hot rice. May be served with "chili vinegar sauce" (P.11).

● See Fig.1 for 2 .

Fig.1

叉燒肉燴飯
Roast Pork over Rice

豬肉(厚5公分)…………8兩

1
白醬油 ……………… 1½大匙
海鮮醬(圖1)………1½大匙
甜醬油 ……………… 1小匙

2
胡椒 ……………… ¼小匙
水 ……………… ½杯
太白粉 ……………… ½大匙

飯 ……………… 2杯

⅔ lb. (300g) pork,
  2″(5cm) thick

1
1½ T. ea: thin soy sauce,
  Hoisin sauce (Fig.1)
1 t. sweet soy sauce

2
¼ t. pepper
½ c. water
½ T. cornstarch

2 c. cooked rice

1 用叉子在肉四週打洞，拌入 1 料(圖2)醃15分鐘後置烤架上。烤箱燒熱以400° F烤50分鐘至肉熟，取出切片，肉汁留用。

2 將肉汁、醃肉汁與 2 料拌勻燒開後，淋在飯或肉片上，可與「辣椒魚露」(見 11頁)配食。

1 Use fork to make holes all over pork then marinate in 1 15 minutes (Fig.2). Bake pork in 400°F oven 50 minutes until cooked, remove and cut in pieces. Reserve liquid.

2 Mix reserved liquid, marinade, and 2 completely, then bring to a boil; pour mixture over rice or meat. Tastes best when served with "chili fish sauce" (P.11).

Fig. 1

Fig.2

Fig.3

雞肉燴飯
Spicy Chicken with Chili & Basil over Rice

	雞肉(切條) ·················	8兩
1	蒜末 ······················	1小匙
	辣椒(切絲) ··············	6條
2	魚露 ······················	1½大匙
	甜醬油 ····················	1½小匙
	糖 ·························	½小匙
3	九層塔 ····················	20片
	高湯(或水) ··············	⅓杯
	飯 ·························	2杯

⅔ lb. (300g) boneless
  chicken, cut in strips

1 · 1 t. minced garlic
    6 shredded chilies

2 · 1½ T. fish sauce
    1½ t. sweet soy sauce
    ½ t. sugar

3 · 20 basil leaves
    ⅓ c. stock or water

2 c. cooked rice

1 油2大匙燒熱，炒香 1 料、隨入肉炒熟，續入 2 料拌炒後，再加 3 料燒開，澆在飯上即成。

1 Heat 2 T. oil then stir-fry 1 until fragrant. Add meat and stir-fry until color changes. Add 2 ; stir to mix. Add 3 and bring to boil. Pour on rice; serve.

辣味雞炒飯
Spicy Chicken with Fried Rice

	雞肉(切條) ·················	6兩
	四季豆(切段) ··············	1杯
1	1 料同上	
	飯 ·························	2杯
2	2 料同上	
	九層塔 ····················	12片

½ lb. (225g) boneless
  chicken, cut in strips
1 c. string beans, cut
  2″ (5cm) long

1 · see 1 in above recipe

2 c. cooked rice

2 · see 2 in above recipe

12 basil leaves

1 油2大匙燒熱、炒香 1 料，隨入雞肉、四季豆炒至肉熟，依序入飯、 2 料及九層塔拌炒均勻即成。

● 雞肉、四季豆(見84頁，圖3)。

1 Heat 2 T. oil then stir-fry 1 until fragrant. Add chicken and string beans; stir-fry until meat changes color. Add rice, 2 and basil leaves; stir-fry and mix well. Serve.

● See Fig.3, P.84 for chicken and string beans.

蝦仁炒飯
Shrimp & Fried Rice

蝦（無殼）·····················6兩

1｜蒜末·····················½小匙
　｜洋葱末····················¼杯

蛋······················2個
飯······················2杯

2｜青豆仁····················3大匙
　｜葱花·····················2大匙

3｜魚露·····················1½大匙
　｜蠔油·····················½大匙
　｜糖······················½小匙

青檸檬····················½個

½ lb. (225g) shelled shrimp

1｜½ t. minced garlic
　｜¼ c. minced onion

2 eggs
2 c. cooked rice

2｜3 T. green peas
　｜2 T. chopped green onion

3｜1½ T. fish sauce
　｜½ T. oyster sauce
　｜½ t. sugar

½ lime

1 蝦抽去腸泥，洗淨後瀝乾水份。

2 油2大匙燒熱，炒香**1**料，隨入蝦炒熟，續入蛋炒至略乾，依序入飯及**2**、**3**料拌炒後，淋上青檸檬汁即成。

● 讀者可利用身邊有的材料及剩餘的飯，做出各種不同口味香噴噴的泰式炒飯。亦可參考85、87頁。

1 Devein shrimp; rinse and drain.

2 Heat 2 T. oil then stir-fry **1** until fragrant. Add shrimp and stir-fry until color changes. Add eggs and stir-fry until slightly solid. Add rice, **2**, then **3**; stir to mix. Squeeze on lime juice. Serve.

● For different flavored Thai fried rice, use any available ingredients and leftover rice. See P.85 and P.87 for reference.

Fig.1　　　　　　　　　　　Fig.2

鳳梨蝦炒飯
Pineapple Shrimp & Fried Rice

蝦（無殼） ···················· 6兩

<u>1</u> 蒜末、大蝦膏········· 各1小匙
　 辣椒（切絲） ·············· 4條

　 飯 ························· 2杯
　 新鮮或罐裝鳳梨（切塊）···½杯

<u>2</u> 魚露 ····················· 2大匙
　 糖 ·······················½小匙

<u>3</u> 葱花、腰果··············各¼杯

½ lb. (225g) shelled shrimp

<u>1</u> 1 t. ea: minced garlic,
　 shrimp paste with soya
　 bean oil
　 4 shredded chilies

　 2 c. cooked rice
　 ½ c. fresh or canned
　 pineapple pieces

<u>2</u> 2 T. fish sauce
　 ½ t. sugar

<u>3</u> ¼ c. ea: chopped green
　 onions, cashew nuts

1 蝦抽去腸泥，洗淨後瀝乾水份。

2 油2大匙燒熱，炒香<u>1</u>料，隨入蝦炒熟，依序入飯、鳳梨及<u>2</u>、<u>3</u>料炒拌均勻即成。

● 大蝦膏見86頁圖1。如無大蝦膏時可用蟹膏來取代。

1 Devein shrimp; rinse and drain.

2 Heat 2 T. oil then stir-fry <u>1</u> until fragrant. Add shrimp and stir-fry until color changes. Add rice, pineapple pieces, <u>2</u>, then <u>3</u>; stir well to mix. Serve.

● Crab paste with soya bean oil may be substituted for shrimp paste with soya bean oil. (Fig. 1, P.86)

豬肉炒飯
Pork & Fried Rice

豬肉（切片、見86頁，圖2）···6兩

<u>1</u> 蒜末 ····················· 1小匙
　 洋葱絲 ·····················¼杯

　 蛋 ························· 2個
　 飯 ························· 2杯

<u>2</u> <u>2</u>料同上

<u>3</u> 葱花、番茄丁············各¼杯

　 青檸檬 ·····················½個

½ lb. (225g) sliced pork
(Fig.2, P.86)

<u>1</u> 1 t. minced garlic
　 ¼ c. shredded onion

　 2 eggs，2 c. cooked rice

<u>2</u> see <u>2</u> in above recipe

<u>3</u> ¼ c. ea (chopped): tomato,
　 green onions

　 ½ lime

1 油2大匙燒熱，炒香<u>1</u>料，隨入肉炒熟、續入蛋炒至略乾，依序入飯及<u>2</u>、<u>3</u>料拌炒後，淋上青檸檬汁即成。可與「辣椒魚露」（見11頁）配食。

● 忙碌的的職業婦女如用絞肉來取代肉片，做出來的飯也同樣好吃。

1 Heat 2 T. oil then stir-fry <u>1</u> until fragrant. Add meat and stir-fry until color changes. Add eggs and stir-fry until slightly solid. Add rice, <u>2</u>, then <u>3</u>; stir to mix. Squeeze on lime juice. May be served with "chili fish sauce" (P.11).

● To save time for busy working pepole, ground pork may be used to make equally delicious fried rice.

炸香蕉
Fried Bananas

香蕉（切段）················ 3根
麵粉 ····················· 8大匙

1 鹽 ·····················⅛小匙
   糖 ····················· 1大匙
   椰奶漿或牛奶 ·········· 4大匙
   蛋（打散）·············· 1個

2 椰子粉絲 ················ 2杯
   芝麻 ···················· 2大匙

炸油·····················適量

3 bananas, cut in sections
8 T. flour

1 ⅛ t. salt
   1 T. sugar
   4 T. thick coconut milk or
      milk
   1 beaten egg

2 2 c. sweetened coconut,
      shredded
   2 T. sesame seeds

oil for deep-frying

1 ①料打勻，加入麵粉拌成軟硬適中的麵糊；香蕉先沾麵糊，再邊沾邊捏至充分裹上②料（圖1）。

2 炸油燒熱，放入備好香蕉，炸至金黃色撈出，置於紙巾上吸油，置盤食用。

● 太生的香蕉味不甜，太熟的做時容易爛，故選購時以熟度適中爲宜。

● 香蕉沾裹②料後可冰凍保存，食時解凍再炸。

1 Stir ① well then mix with flour to form batter. Dip bananas in batter then coat completely with ② (Fig. 1).

2 Heat oil for deep-frying then fry the coated bananas until golden; remove and place on paper towel to absorb oil. Place bananas on plate; serve.

● Unripe bananas are not sweet; if too ripe they break easily. Therefore, medium ripe bananas should be used in this recipe.

● Bananas coated with ② may be frozen. Defrost bananas then deep-fry when ready to serve.

Fig. 1

Fig. 2

Fig. 3

芒果甜飯
Sweet Rice & Mango

芒果甜飯

長糯米 ‥‥‥‥‥‥‥‥‥‥ 1杯

1 椰奶漿或牛奶‥‥‥‥‥‥‥¼杯
糖 ‥‥‥‥‥‥‥‥‥ 1½大匙

芝麻 ‥‥‥‥‥‥‥‥‥ 1大匙
芒果(切塊) ‥‥‥‥‥‥‥ 1個

1 c. sticky rice

1 **¼ c. thick coconut milk or milk**
1½ T. sugar

1 T. sesame seeds
1 mango, cut in pieces

1 糯米泡水6小時，瀝乾水份，倒入竹籠內(見88頁，圖2)，水燒開將竹籠置上，大火蒸約20分鐘，趁熱拌入 1 料，食時撒上芝麻與芒果配食。

● 竹籠是泰式蒸飯特殊道具，若無時可用蒸籠或電鍋取代。

1 Soak sticky rice 6 hours in cold water. Drain, then pour into bamboo basket (Fig.2, P.88). Put the basket in boiling water; steam in high heat 20 minutes. Remove and mix hot rice with 1 . When serving, sprinkle with sesame seeds and mango.

● Bamboo basket is a special device used in steaming Thai rice. If not available, substitute with steamer or rice cooker.

南瓜甜盅
Steamed Custard in Pumpkin

蛋 ‥‥‥‥‥‥‥‥‥‥ 3個

1 椰奶漿或牛奶‥‥‥‥‥‥‥¼杯
椰子糖 ‥‥‥‥‥‥‥‥‥ 5大匙

南瓜1個 ‥‥‥‥‥‥‥‥ 12兩

3 eggs

1 **¼ c. thick coconut milk or milk**
5 T. palm sugar

1 pumpkin, I lb. (450g)

1 南瓜去頂蓋，去籽，沖洗瀝乾。 1 料打勻至糖溶化，再加蛋拌勻，倒入南瓜內用大火蒸45分鐘至蛋凝固即取出，冰涼後切成楔形食用(見88頁， 圖3)。

1 Remove pumpkin top and seeds; rinse and drain. Beat 1 until sugar dissolves; add eggs and mix well. Pour into pumpkin then steam in high heat 45 minutes until eggs solidify; remove and refrigerate. Cut in triangular pieces (Fig.3, P.88); serve.

椰子蛋塔

Thai Custard

去皮綠豆(圖1) ············· ¼杯
椰奶漿或牛奶 ············· 2杯

1 | 蛋 ···························· 4個
   | 椰子糖 ·················· 10大匙

2 | 椰子粉絲 ················· ¼杯
   | 鹽 ······················· ¼小匙

洋葱(切絲) ·············· 1杯

¼ c. mung beans (Fig.1)
2 c. thick coconut milk or milk

1 | 4 eggs
   | 10 T. palm sugar

2 | ¼ c. sweetened coconut shredded
   | ¼ t. salt

1 c. shredded onion

1 水燒開,放入豆煮約20分鐘至軟,撈出與椰奶漿在果汁機內攪爛成豆奶。

2 1料打勻與豆奶、2料用小火邊煮邊攪至呈濃稠狀,倒入烤盤內以350°F烤45分鐘後,再用500°F續烤5分鐘取出。

3 油1杯燒熱,用中火將洋葱炸呈棕色撈出,置於紙巾上吸油,撒在蛋塔上(圖2),待涼後切塊。

1 Cook beans in boiling water 20 minutes until soft. Remove and liquify with thick coconut milk in a blender to make bean milk.

2 Mix 1 well then cook with bean milk and 2 in low heat until thick, stirring during cooking. Pour into baking plate then bake at 350°F 45 minutes. Continue baking at 500°F 5 minutes. Remove.

3 Heat 1 c. oil for deep-frying then fry onion over medium heat until color changes to brown. Remove and place on paper towel to absorb oil. Sprinkle onion on custard (Fig.2). Let cool completely, then cut in pieces.

Fig. 1

Fig. 2

Fig. 3

Fig. 4

黑糖豆腐花湯
Tofu Pudding

豆腐花(見90頁,圖3)⋯⋯⋯8兩

1
水 ⋯⋯⋯⋯⋯⋯⋯⋯⋯ 2杯
薑(洗淨、略拍)⋯⋯⋯⅔兩
黑糖 ⋯⋯⋯⋯⋯⋯⋯ 7大匙

餛飩皮 ⋯⋯⋯⋯⋯⋯⋯ 2張
炸油⋯⋯⋯⋯⋯⋯⋯⋯⋯適量

⅔ lb. (300g)fresh soy bean
   pudding (Fig.3, P.90)

1
2 c. water
1 oz. (28g) ginger, lightly
   crushed
7 T. brown sugar

2 won ton skins
oil for deep-frying

1 炸油燒熱,餛飩皮用中火炸至金黃色,撈出略壓碎,備用。

2 ①料燒開後煮約5分鐘,用大湯匙將豆腐花一片片舀入甜湯內燒熱(若煮太久豆腐會老,不好吃),撒上碎餛飩皮即成。

1 Heat oil for deep-frying then fry won ton skins in medium heat until golden. Remove and slightly crush the skin; set aside.

2 Bring ① to boil then cook 5 minutes. Use large spoon to spoon pudding, slice by slice, into ①; cook until hot. Do not overcook. Sprinkle with crushed won ton skins. Serve.

芋頭南瓜甜湯
Taro & Pumpkin in Coconut Milk

芋頭、南瓜切塊 ⋯⋯⋯ 各3兩
(見90頁,圖4)

1
椰奶漿 ⋯⋯⋯⋯⋯⋯⋯ 1½杯
椰子糖 ⋯⋯⋯⋯⋯⋯⋯ 3大匙

¼ lb. (115g) ea (cut in pieces):
   taro, pumpkin
   (Fig.4, P.90)

1
1½ c. thick coconut milk
3 T. palm sugar

1 將芋頭與南瓜放入①料內燒開,用小火煮10分鐘至軟即成。

● 芋頭與南瓜任選一種,即可煮成芋頭甜湯或南瓜甜湯;此為一道簡單易做的飯後甜湯。

1 Add taro and pumpkin to ① then bring to boil. Reduce to low heat and cook 10 minutes until tender.

● Taro and pumpkin may be used together, or individually depending on personal preference.

冰咖啡
Thai Ice Coffee

☐1 泰式咖啡粉(圖1)
　　或普通咖啡粉 ……… 4大匙
　水 …………………… 2杯

☐2 糖 …………………… 4大匙
　煉乳(圖2) …………… 4大匙

　奶水(圖2) …………… 適量

☐1 4 T. Thai coffee (Fig.1) or
　regular coffee
　2 c. water

☐2 4 T. sugar
　4 T. sweetened condensed
　milk (Fig.2)

　half and half as desired
　(Fig.2)

1 將☐1料放入咖啡器內濾煮過，可煮約1¾杯，隨入☐2料拌勻冰涼備用。

2 食時杯內各裝¾杯的冰塊，再加煮好的的咖啡及奶水即成。

● 黑咖啡：將煮好的咖啡加6大匙糖攪拌冰涼，食時倒入有冰塊的杯內即成。

● 如用即溶咖啡粉時，按包裝指示沖泡1¾杯咖啡再依上列做法做成冰咖啡。

1 Brew ☐1 by coffee maker to make 1¾ c. coffee. Dissolve ☐2 in coffee. Refrigerate.

2 When serving, put ¾ c. ice in each glass. Add brewed coffee then half and half.

● Black Coffee: Dissolve 6T. sugar in 1¾ c. brewed coffee then refrigerate. When serving , pour ice then coffee into glass.

● If using instant coffee, follow package instructions to prepare 1¾ c.coffee then follow the above procedures.

Fig. 1

Fig. 2

冰茶
Thai Ice Tea

<table>
<tr><td>1</td><td>泰式茶粉（圖1）⋯⋯⋯⋯4大匙
水 ⋯⋯⋯⋯⋯⋯⋯⋯⋯ 2杯</td></tr>
<tr><td>2</td><td>糖 ⋯⋯⋯⋯⋯⋯⋯⋯⋯ 4大匙
煉乳（見92頁，圖2）⋯⋯4大匙</td></tr>
<tr><td></td><td>奶水（見92頁，圖2）⋯⋯ 適量</td></tr>
</table>

1 4 T. Thai tea (Fig.1)
  2 c. water

2 4 T. sugar
  4 T. sweetened condensed
     milk (P.92, Fig.2)

  half and half as desired
     (P.92, Fig.2)

1 將1料放入咖啡器內濾煮過，可煮約1¾杯，隨入2料拌勻冰涼備用。

2 食時杯內各裝¾杯的冰塊，再加煮好的茶及奶水即成。

● 檸檬茶：將煮好的茶加入6大匙糖，攪拌冰涼，食時倒入有冰塊的杯內，加少許檸檬汁即成。

● 普通的茶，略泡濃些亦可用來調製冰茶，不同種類的茶，各有不同的風味。

1 Brew 1 by coffee maker to make 1¾ c. tea. Dissolve 2 in tea. Refrigerate.

2 When serving, put ¾ c. ice in each glass. Add the brewed tea then half and half.

● Lemon Tea: Dissolve 6T. sugar in brewed tea then refrigerate. When serving, pour ice then tea into glass.

● If using other kinds of tea, follow package instructions and prepare slightly darker. Different teas provide different flavors.

Fig. 1

索　引

INDEX